Effective Differentiation

Packed full of prompts, activities and practical ideas, this accessible and realistic guide provides teachers with a rich portfolio of strategies to ensure inclusion, and promote the learning of Special Educational Needs (SEN) pupils in the mainstream classroom.

Unpacking SEN, demystifying jargon, and clarifying policy and good practice, *Effective Differentiation* encourages its reader to take a proactive approach to developing knowledge and skills in relation to Special Educational Needs Disability (SEND). Chapters address the challenges involved in successfully differentiating teaching to meet the diverse needs of individual children, and translate current research and policy into easy-to-understand concepts, integrating these into a framework for practical application. Taking self-evaluation as a starting point, the reader is invited to think, reflect, understand and finally – do!

The perfect aid for the busy teacher, each chapter contains checklists and photocopiable tables which readers can use to record and track their own progress.

Abigail Gray has more than 20 years of experience in SEN, as a specialist teacher, SEN co-ordinator (SENCO) and school leader. She now works both as a private SEND consultant and trainer for her own company, Senworks Ltd, and as an Achievement Coach for the educational charity Achievement for All.

Effective Differentiation

A Training Guide to Empower Teachers and Enable Learners with SEND and Specific Learning Difficulties

Abigail Gray

Routledge
Taylor & Francis Group

LONDON AND NEW YORK

First published 2018
by Routledge
2 Park Square, Milton Park, Abingdon, Oxon OX14 4RN

and by Routledge
711 Third Avenue, New York, NY 10017

Routledge is an imprint of the Taylor & Francis Group, an informa business

British Library Cataloguing-in-Publication Data
A catalogue record for this book is available from the British Library

Library of Congress Cataloging-in-Publication Data
A catalog record for this book has been requested

ISBN: 978-1-138-50282-6 (hbk)
ISBN: 978-1-138-50283-3 (pbk)
ISBN: 978-1-315-14509-9 (ebk)

Typeset in Sabon
by Apex CoVantage, LLC

Visit the eResources: www.routledge.com/9781138502833

To my mother and father
Frances and Percy Gray

Contents

3   How do I identify learners with SEND? The Needs Matrix   31

4   What are 'core deficits'?   47

Acknowledgements

I'd like to thank all my teachers. Jane Luckman who coaxed me out of my shell as a tot, Lucy Cornish who made me laugh and helped me to be less anxious about school, Barbara Smith who recognised my ability and made sure my teenage years were not entirely wasted on Wham, John Picton whose persistence and encouragement almost convinced me of a life in academia, Joan Lumley who is still the best Head of Learning Support I have ever met, Elizabeth James, my role model for women in leadership and Robert Carlysle who embodies the character and values of a great Head Teacher.

An extra special note of sincere thanks to the unstintingly generous Robert Carlysle and his wife, Terry, who have given so much of their time and energy to me during this project.

Thanks also to all the teachers, support staff and school leaders I have had the privilege of working alongside, in every capacity, over the last 25 years. I never cease to be amazed by the energy, commitment, devotion and patience of the people in this profession.

Finally, thanks to my husband, James, for his love, unwavering support and creativity and to my amazing daughter, Mim, who is both my inspiration and my foundation.

Introduction

Every chapter and every section of the book is written in response to a hypothetical question phrased in the first person: 'What do I know . . .?', 'How can I make . . .?' For this purpose, 'I' indicates the reader and most often assumes the reader to be a teacher in training or practice. The 'I' questions that follow are the ones I asked myself before beginning this piece of work.

What am I trying to achieve in writing this book?

In November 2017 the BBC revealed the results of their investigation into the numbers of home-educated pupils with Special Educational Needs (SEN). Data from 106 Local Authorities about pupils supported by Education, Health and Care Plans showed a 57% increase (over a five-year period)[1] in parents choosing home education for their children, with an even greater increase in England than in Wales or Northern Ireland. The media narrative accompanying these statistics revealed the individual stories of increasing numbers of parents preferring to upend their own lives and make special educational provision for their children at home rather than to rely on schools to make the special provision required.

Most of my working life, in both mainstream and special schools, has been spent teaching pupils with SEN. Each day has provided me with an opportunity to experience and to try to understand the ways children with SEN struggle with school. During more than a decade of leadership in a specialist setting for pupils with specific learning difficulties (SpLDs), I met hundreds of children and parents who had lost their faith in education and educators. These children had often been through a rigorous process of assessment beginning with the often-painful recognition that 'something was wrong'. Families don't rush towards special provision; they want their children to learn and thrive in the same way as anyone else. Families came to our small school exhausted by what they saw as the failure of mainstream education to make the necessary special provision for their child.

It is important to recognise that in making a special educational provision for difficulties with learning there must be room for the recognition of ability. The discourse around neurodiversity is proliferating but finds little practical expression in the way schools manage Special Educational Needs Disability (SEND) provision. Pupils with learning difficulties are also pupils with learning abilities.

Who is it for?

However, this is not a book about special schools for specialists; it's a book which explores how specialist educational knowledge can inform and enhance mainstream educational provision. It's a book for mainstream teachers, designed to lay the groundwork in terms of their knowledge about SEN.

The book is structured in consideration of the 2016 Standards for Teachers' Continuing Professional Development,[2] acknowledging the role of the school in establishing a consistent approach to training and development, the model here is to support the teacher directly and to encourage proactivity in developing the necessary knowledge and skills about SEND.

What does it do?

My aim in putting it together was to create a pocket specialist, a supportive guide to use when thinking about SEN and teaching pupils with learning difficulties.

Over the last four years while working as a trainer and consultant, I found myself receiving repeated requests from school leaders asking for training on 'the basics', a SEN bitesize or a starter pack for beginners. This is my response; it recognises the need to make a direct link between academic study, research and its practical application.

The process of writing prompted me to ask questions about why teachers might read books about education and pedagogy. Indeed, it made me think about what I had read as a newly qualified teacher and during my teaching career. I found that generally teachers read about practice for three reasons: because someone they know and/or respect has made a recommendation; because a book touches on an area of interest or a problem they are struggling to overcome; and as part of a formal course of study. Irrespective of what leads me to read it, a book really stays with me only if, in some way, it changes me, if it opens a new vista into a world I inhabit or into my inner world. Like reading, professional training experiences would appear to stick only where they touch. No matter how noble the ultimate aims, the session will have limited effect without a specific and personal motivation to do something as a result. With this consideration in mind, this book is full of ideas but also full of prompts to think and to do.

Acknowledging the fact that your school requires you to develop strategies to manage the diverse needs of pupils in the classroom from the outset and to take responsibility for the impact of that teaching, I wanted to create a book that encouraged activity not passivity, a book about SEN to use, rather than to read. Therefore, this is a workbook rather than an academic treatise, and it requires a degree of interaction. In reading and working through this book it's possible to record and track your understanding and practice as it develops.

How does it do it?

During the Wimbledon fortnight I become briefly but passionately engaged in tennis. Last year I found myself contemplating the wonder of Federer: his superhuman ability to place the perfect shot and his power and grace in managing whatever came back at him. Briefly transfixed by the slick, computer graphics displayed on screen during the match, I quickly found myself irritated and more than a little resentful. For the benefit of a game, technology has managed to produce computer analytics capable of describing every possible nuance of action and environment. I found myself wishing for a graphic illustrating the speed, the impact and the trajectory of approaches to teaching and learning. Teachers, like tennis players, are judged on performance, but sadly they must hone their skills without a team of physios, coaches ,and all the digital paraphernalia that 21st-century technology has to offer. Teaching skill is still assessed via a combination of largely subjective forms of feedback, working towards the ultimate game, set and match of lesson observations, exam results and staying power – not a strawberry in sight.

Successfully differentiating teaching to include pupils with SEND in a mainstream classroom, like any other aspect of teaching, is likely to be hard work. Policy documents, books and articles that claim otherwise are entirely misleading. A school's SEND provision may appear to be discrete and to occupy the same theoretical and physical space as any other department. It may have a suite of rooms, a team of staff, a set of resources and a budget like English or Geography – but unlike any other department it doesn't function like a limb. It can't be isolated and reset in the same way. The SEND provision is an interconnected system of processes and provisions that express a school's attitude to pupils with SpLD and SEND. How effectively teachers fulfil their role and adapt their teaching for pupils with SEND is a vital measure of the overall effectiveness of the provision. This book is designed to help teachers become more aware of their existing approaches to teaching pupils with SEND and offers a framework for improving with self-evaluation as a starting point.

Throughout the book you are invited to consider the ideas and material from a personal perspective and to reflect on your own experience.

How do I manage SEN jargon and terminology?

In writing a book aimed teachers, rather than SEN co-ordinators (SENCOs), one over-arching aim is to unpack SEN jargon and clarify the relevant terminology required for good practice.

SEND has become an acronym with powerful connotations as an indicator of disadvantage. 'Learning difficulty', 'disability' and 'special needs' are often used interchangeably. The first chapter of the book deals with the origins of these terms and clarifies their meaning and the relationship between them. Following chapters explain the distinctions inherent in the description of a SpLD. I have used all the terms in the book but have endeavoured to do so consistently and specifically.

For the purposes of this book, the word 'differentiation' is a shorthand for teaching that actively acknowledges and respects diversity – teaching that enables access, considers individuals, includes and thinks seriously about challenge.

When referring to school-age children in the school setting I have used the word 'pupils' but accept that many teachers refer to students.

The assumed audience is teachers of pupils attending mainstream schools in both primary and secondary phase, in the maintained or independent sector. While the teaching methods covered may have relevance to Early Years, Further and Higher Education settings these are not my areas of specialism or experience.

Where technical language has been used, an attempt has been made to explain and illustrate its use and meaning.

A final word about the notion of SEND as a category. While it is essential that schools collect and analyse data about the performance of groups of children, it's helpful to remember that the word 'analysis' comes from the Greek word *lysis*, meaning 'to split'. As teachers, the way we break things down isn't necessarily the way we build things up. The acronyms we use to describe disadvantaged pupils describe a circumstance, not a person, just like the labels we might ascribe to a pupil's specific learning exist to describe the difficulty, not the child. We analyse the information not to excuse or explain a problem but to help us to find the best ways to mitigate it and let children into school-based learning at its fullest and its best.

Notes

1 See also www.bbc.co.uk/news/education-42103248
2 Standard for teachers' professional development Implementation guidance for school leaders, teachers, and organisations that offer professional development for teachers.

Chapter 1

What do I know about Special Educational Needs Disability and inclusive teaching?

This chapter provides the reader with an opportunity to deepen their understanding of inclusive teaching and to identify their aspirations in regard to classroom practice. It provides a summary of the educational, legal and political framework for inclusive education and sets current practice into the broader context, referring to the history of inclusion for students with Special Educational Needs Disability (SEND).

This chapter invites the reader to start work, and to reflect on their school's arrangements for SEND, inclusive teaching and differentiation.

When I first walked into a classroom in 1991 I was entirely unaware of the Special Educational Needs (SEN) system. I had an awareness of disability and had come across SpLDs like dyslexia but was not aware of how teaching could be modified to enable such learners to succeed. I was starting from scratch in a way that it would be hard to replicate today. With no internet, no social media and nothing like the public and political awareness about SEND that surrounds classroom practice today, it was not uncommon for teachers to be similarly unfamiliar with this aspect of education.

The knowledge and experience I have gained since then can be roughly divided into four main areas: the law, leadership and management of SEND, specialist approaches to teaching and learning, and working with children and families. While no classroom teacher necessarily needs to become an expert in all four, having some awareness of the way the system has evolved and its legal structure is a distinct advantage and underpins good practice.

Why is the law relating to SEND relevant for classroom teachers?

As a school-wide provision, rather than a traditional department, school arrangements for SEND lack the usual curricular structure which underpins other school departments. Its constitution and principles are constructed by educational law and the official guidance about implementation produced by the Department for Education (DFE).

The Code of Practice refers to the commitment of the UK Government to the 'inclusive education of disabled children and young people and the progressive removal of barriers to learning and participation in mainstream education' under articles 7 and 24 of the United Nations Convention of the Rights of Persons with Disabilities (DFE, 2015, pp. 1.26, 25).

The right to a mainstream education for children with SEN was first described in legal terms relatively recently. Following the Warnock report of 1978 and inclusions in the subsequent Education Acts of 1981 and 1993, the existing definitions relating to SEND were finally consolidated into the Education Act of 1996; this has recently been superseded by the Children and Family Act 2014 (CAFA).

CAFA sets out explicit duties in respect of children with SEN or disabilities. School duties, along with those of Local Authorities and other organisations, are set out in the Special Educational Needs and Disability Code of Practice: 0–25 years (Code of Practice) which relates directly to CAFA.

The Code of Practice took effect on September 1st 2014 and details statutory guidance to organisations, including schools, relating to young people with SEND.

It relates to Part 3 of CAFA along with other regulations (DFE, 2015, p. 12).

The Code of Practice refers to the statutory duties placed on organisations regarding disabled children and young people by the Equality Act 2010 (DFE, 2015, p. 16).

Forming an understanding of the key definitions contained in CAFA is an essential, but often overlooked, starting point for teachers. The terms 'learning difficulty', 'disability', 'special educational needs' and 'special educational provision' are interrelated but not interchangeable.

The definitions of a *special education need, a learning difficulty* and *special educational provision*, along with a definition of *disability* are as follows.

Definition of SEN

Section 20 (1) of CAFA

A child or young person has SEN if they have a learning difficulty or disability which calls for special educational provision to be made for them.

Definition of a learning difficulty

Section 20 (2) of CAFA

A child of compulsory school age or a young person has a learning difficulty or disability if they:

(a) have a significantly greater difficulty in learning than *the majority of others of the same age*; or
(b) have a disability which prevents or hinders them from making use of educational facilities *of a kind generally provided for others of the same age in mainstream schools or mainstream post-16 institutions.*

Special Educational Provision

Section 21 of CAFA

(1) 'Special educational provision', for a child aged two or more or a young person, means educational or training provision that is additional to, or different from, that made generally for others of the same age in—

(a) mainstream schools in England,

(b) maintained nursery schools in England,

(c) mainstream post-16 institutions in England, or

(d) places in England at which relevant early years education is provided.

Disability

Section 6 (1) of the Equality Act 2010

A person (P) has a disability for the purposes of this Act if:

- P has a physical or mental impairment; and
- the impairment has a substantial and long-term adverse effect on P's ability to carry out normal day-to-day activities. (Section 6),

The Code of Practice explains the relationship between SEN, special educational provision and disability (DFE, 2015, pp. xviii, 16). A learning difficulty may or may not constitute a disability and in either case may or may not result in SEN and the implementation of a special educational provision.

Three principles underpinning the Code of Practice, taken from Section 19 of the Children and Families Act 2014, are set out in detail in Chapter 1 (see DFE, 2015, pp. 1.1, 19). In brief, Local Authorities take the following into consideration in carrying out functions under the Act:

- the voice of pupils and their families;
- support for participation of pupils and families in decision-making processes; and
- support for child facilitating successful outcomes in terms of educational achievement and preparation for adulthood.

In respect to schools, the Code of Practice refers to eight sections of legislation The Equality Act 2010 and the Special Educational Needs and Disability Regulations 2014, as the relevant primary legislation. The Code refers to statutory responsibilities placed upon schools[1] in terms of duties they 'must' perform.

As well as being required to identify and address the SEN of the pupils that they support, these 'must' duties include:

- use their best endeavours to make sure that a child with SEN gets the support they need – this means doing everything they can to meet children and young people's SEN
- ensure that children and young people with SEN engage in the activities of the school alongside pupils who do not have SEN
- designate a teacher to be responsible for co-ordinating SEN provision – the SEN co-ordinator, or SENCO (this does not apply to 16 to 19 academies)

- inform parents when they are making special educational provision for a child
- prepare an SEN information report and their arrangements for the admission of disabled children, the steps being taken to prevent disabled children from being treated less favourably than others, the facilities provided to enable access to the school for disabled children and their accessibility plan showing how they plan to improve access progressively over time

(DFE, 2015, p. 92)

When successfully applied, the Act and the guidance to schools provided in the Code of Practice sets out a process designed to enable pupils with SEND (whether or not they are in receipt of an Education, Health and Care [EHC] plan) to access an appropriate education, 'achieve their best' (DFE, 2015, p. 92) and make a successful transition to the next stage of their lives with confidence.

The principles are designed to support 7 outcomes in terms of practice: participation of children and families, early identification and support, choice, collaboration across services, high quality provision, inclusive practice and successful preparation for adulthood (DFE, 2015, pp. 1.2, 19).

What is an Education, Health and Care plan?

When a school finds it cannot make the appropriate provision for a child's SEN, an application can be made to the relevant Local Authority to conduct a statutory assessment.[2] When a process of statutory assessment results in an Education, Health and Care Plan it should reflect a coordinated approach across the educational, social and health care sectors and fully address a child's SEN. This process and the plan that results should be clear and detailed in every respect. It should describe the child's learning difficulties and SENs, the setting and provision required and the details of additional curricular or specialist therapeutic support, as well as the details of any social or health care provision. (See details of the EHC plan in Chapter 2, Figure 2.1.)

A parent, a young person, or a school may request that their Local Authority make a Statutory Assessment of a child's SEN. The Local Authority must respond to the request within a six-week period, either agreeing or refusing to carry out the assessment.

How many school pupils have an EHC plan?

Statistics on SEN for England published in January 2017 (DFE, 2017) recorded that 242,185 pupils were in receipt of an EHC plan or a Statement of Special Educational Needs; that's 2.8% of the total pupil population.

Following a successful initial application, the statutory assessment process is highly likely to result in a EHC plan (previously a Statement); last year, 95.6% of those statutory assessments resulted in a EHC plan.

Unfortunately, this statistic does not tell the whole story. Despite the clarification of rights and duties in law, the experience for families and schools is often complicated and bureaucratic, ending in disappointment. Statutory Assessment is something of a bottleneck and large numbers of applications are refused. In the 2016–17 academic year Local

Authorities refused to assess more than one third of the applications made. In 14,795 cases the opportunity of assessment was denied, which represented a 35.3% increase in refusals to assess since the previous year. It is worth noting that the initial application is a rigorous process, prompted by the concerns of schools and families who consider the educational provision available falls short (DFE, 2017, p. 8).

The process of statutory assessment can sorely test the resilience of schools and families. As a result, a system designed to protect the rights of children and young people with SEN to a mainstream education has too often become a serious bone of contention for children and families, schools and authorities, resulting in disagreements that require professional mediation or referral to the First-Tier Tribunal.

Numbers of pupils supported by EHC plans are significantly smaller than those identified in schools as SEN Support.

A Statutory Assessment is very likely to lead to the creation of an EHC plan.

Local Authorities refuse to assess a significant proportion of pupils following the initial application.

What about pupils with SEN who don't have EHC plans?

The vast majority of school-age children with SEN are not in receipt of special educational provision via an EHC plan or Statement. Statistics published by the DFE in 2017 showed that 1,002,070 pupils were recorded on school registers of SEN as receiving SEN support. This was equal to 11.6% of the total pupil population. (DFE, 2017) The needs of these pupils were considered to be within the compass of the existing whole-school SEN provision. These pupils rely upon the ability of school leaders to identify and designate the appropriate resources to support them and teachers to make the necessary adaptations to teaching to meet their educational needs.

What is the Special Educational Needs and Disability Tribunal (SENDIST)?

When Local Authorities make decisions regarding SEND, parents, young people and authorities sometimes fail to come to an agreement. In specific circumstances, parents have the right to appeal the First-Tier Tribunal (Special Educational Needs and Disability), otherwise known as SENDIST. The appeal can relate to decisions about the process of: carrying out, issuing, amending, re-assessing or maintaining an EHC plan; or pertain to specific aspects of the EHC plan's contents. SENDIST is a chamber of the First-Tier Tribunal and as such is part of the UK court system.

Whilst it is unlikely that a classroom teacher would be asked to attend a Tribunal, it is perhaps valuable to note that it's not unusual for school information and reports to be included in the evidence submitted. My experience as an expert witness and parental representative in SENDIST illustrates the importance of the accuracy and reliability of teacher feedback. Fair decisions can be made only in the light of reliable reporting on a child's attainment and progress. It is always sobering to recognise the breadth of the audience for a teacher's professional opinion and the assessment data that teachers collect. It goes beyond the child, their family and the team at school. As soon as you step into the classroom, you are potentially part of this process.

What are the obligations and structures of 'inclusive' teaching?

The inclusion of children and young people with SEND in mainstream education is the aspiration of an education system that promotes equality under the law and mainstream education as a right and an option for all. However almost 40 years after the Warnock report a practical model for successful inclusion has not been perfected. Alternative and/ or specialist provision is sometimes the preferred option and in certain circumstances the only option. The Green Paper of 2011 (DFE, 2011) identified key faults in a system which limited parental choice of schools, identified children too late, left children out of post-16 education and training, and was overly complex and bureaucratic.

CAFA and the Code of Practice that flows from it are designed to address the issues outlined earlier (amongst other things) by allowing schools greater autonomy and emphasizing the need for staff training.

The ideology of inclusion remains intact but clearly has required repeated revision, particularly in the respects outlined earlier and to ensure the voice of the child and family are heard and their views are included in planning for a successful education and an independent future.

The 'graduated approach' of Assess, Plan, Do, Review (DFE, 2015, p. 100) should ensure that all reasonable measures are taken to assure all pupils with SEN have access to and can succeed within the curriculum. It sets out an evidence-based cycle where teachers continuously review the impact of adapted planning and teaching on pupil progress and attainment, thus identifying, employing and refining the most successful strategies and a personalised approach.

Aspirations for schools and teachers are consistently high. They are expected to be responsive and flexible in differentiating to meet the needs of pupils with SEND and to accurately track the success of provision. Good practice in this respect is essential if schools are to ensure that educational opportunity for children with SEND is real, and that parents and young people have access to the necessary information to make appropriate choices.

My embarrassingly simple observation is that the guidance in the Code of Practice is easy enough to articulate but rather more difficult to implement. Every word of the tidy quartet – Assess, Plan, Do, Review – requires a specific answer to these questions: What? When? How? Assess what? Assess when? Assess how? A successful inclusive teacher is one who understands their role in implementing the school's SEND provision and seeks answers to these far-reaching questions.

How much do you know about your school's approach to and provision for pupils with SEN?

I have selected only some key information that is of relevance for classroom teachers. However, reference to the school's own policies and documentation relating to their arrangements for SEND is essential and a close reading of the relevant section of the Code of Practice (DFE, 2015) is advisable.

The first important step is to acknowledge what you don't know or are unsure about; it's much better to ask a question than to take a position too quickly or act on an assumption. You may be enviably confident about your subject knowledge and specialism, but every class of pupils presents a unique opportunity to understand something more about teaching and learning. The process of teaching children with SEN is a perpetual learning opportunity – to see that as a positive is a good start.

Working through the checklist in Table 1.1 is a handy way to chart your journey into SEND; dating rather than ticking the Yes column could be helpful to you and your SENCO in terms of knowing how well current systems are working.

The graduated approach outlined in the Code of Practice comprises an evidence-based cycle of Assess, Plan, Do, Review.

It's necessary to refer to the school's documentation as approaches to SEND provision, the specifics of SEND management and operations differ from school to school.

Table 1.1 Getting started

Questions	Yes	No	Information/action
Have I read the school SEND policy and or handbook?			
Have I read the school SEND Information report?			
Have I read the school's most recent inspection report or recent performance data?			
Am I aware of the nature of baseline information on *all* pupils in my class?			
Have I met the school SENCO?			
Have I visited any onsite SEND facilities?			
Am I clear about the process of referral?			
Am I clear about channels of communication with SEND staff?			

Self-evaluation

What were the key messages from this chapter?

What do I need to review?

Which activities have I tried?

Which activities would I like to try?

Things I'd like to know more about:

Is this chapter relevant to a specific situation, pupil or class?

Notes

1 Mainstream schools, maintained schools and academies that are not special schools, maintained nursery schools, 16-to-19 academies, alternative provision academies and Pupil Referral Units (PRUs).
2 In 2014 the revised Code of Practice and regulations replaced Statements of Special Educational Needs with Education, Health, and Care plans.

Chapter 2

What about a baseline?

This chapter looks in detail at the variety, content and potential uses of baseline data, offering teachers a structure for thinking through information about ability and attainment in order to enhance teaching practice and pupil attainment. It provides a series of tools to help the teacher to reflect on and to interrogate the available information about their pupils with a focus on developing a better understanding of the relationship between underlying pupil ability and curricula attainment.

It identifies the characteristics and key sources of baseline information with regard to pupils with identified Special Educational Needs Disability (SEND) and highlights the distinctions between the data available for those with Education, Health and Care (EHC) plans, those on Special Educational Needs (SEN) support and those whose needs are yet to be identified.

The chapter considers the role of baseline data in the implementation of the graduated approach of Assess, Plan, Do, Review and unpacks the link between a teacher's knowledge and understanding of baselines and the successful implementation of the cycle.

How can the classroom teacher benefit from the data-rich environment?

Schools have become increasingly data-rich environments, collecting, collating and sorting input using comprehensive, online and intranet-based data management systems. There are often detailed, idiosyncratic protocols and administrators dedicated to recording numerical data about attainment, progress, attendance and behaviour. In addition, contextual data about socio-economic circumstances is used to characterise relationships between indicators of disadvantage and progress and attainment.

Finding meaningful ways to manage complex data about individuals is a key aspect of 21st-century teaching. I think it's true to say that a tension exists between the volume of data generated about individuals and our ability to use it effectively. An intricate web of information is generated around all our pupils, irrespective of their SEND status. The challenge is to find ways to harness the power of this web and to transform it into a supportive net, catching our most vulnerable pupils.

The effectiveness with which the data is interrogated and utilised is obviously a measure of good leadership and planning for school development rather than a matter for class teachers independently. It may be that a forum and structure exist to discuss these data and consider their relevance – but using them informatively, to enhance teaching and learning, can be a challenge for the most experienced practitioner.

What are baseline data?

There is more than one kind of baseline. In common with many other educational terms, 'baseline' can be used to refer to both information on a pupil's curricular progress and attainment and to the scores produced by tests of innate ability and potential.

What's the difference between baseline data derived from standardised tests and data derived from teacher assessment?

Baselines derived from standardised testing provide information about pupil ability calibrated against an age-related national sample and as such have high levels of objectivity and reliability.[1] Standardised scores create parity between scores from tests of different length and duration and consider the age of the pupil at the time of testing. Helpfully, this kind of test and the feedback it provides can be used comparatively alongside other curricular measures of progress and attainment.

The most commonly used tools provide measures of developmental milestones, cognitive ability, numeracy and literacy. There is a plethora of online and paper baselining tools commercially available to schools at every stage, however their use is neither universal nor mandatory.

Tools for baselining pupils in Early Years Education are necessarily different from tests of cognitive abilities for older children as assessments are conducted face to face and include an assessment of the child's development in terms of the social, physical and language skills required for learning. A typical cognitive ability baseline test in a Primary or Secondary setting would most often be conducted in a class group or larger and generate a set of individual and aggregate scores measuring verbal, non-verbal, spatial and numerical reasoning.

What skills do the most widely available standardised baselines relate to?

Reading: It's important to note the aspect of reading ability being measured by the test. In tests of sight reading, such as Wide Range Achievement Test[2] (WRAT) 5 or Salford[3] a pupil might be asked to read single words or sentences aloud so that the pupil's sight vocabulary or ability to decode can be measured. Tests of *reading comprehension* such as NFER Group Reading[4] and the Neale Analysis[5] may require pupils to read whole sentences or paragraphs and to complete sentences by inserting a word from a list or to answer questions about a passage.

Spelling: tests like the Schonell[6] and WRAT5 may generate scores for the whole school or for specific cohorts but generally measure the pupil's ability to listen to a word (in context) and then spell it correctly.

Verbal reasoning scores indicate a pupil's understanding and reasoning ability using words. There are several different types of verbal reasoning questions requiring pupils to demonstrate their knowledge of semantics, vocabulary and the relationships between words.

Non-verbal reasoning scores reveal a pupil's ability to understand, analyse and solve diagrammatic and visual problems using visual reasoning regardless of their linguistic knowledge and skill.

Numerical reasoning scores relate to a pupil's knowledge and understanding of mathematics.

Well-being scales: there may be qualitative information about pupil attitudes to themselves and to school derived from instruments such as the Leuven Scales for Well Being[7] and Involvement or Pupil Attitudes to Self and School (PASS).[8]

From February 2017 there should be details of judgement about language proficiency for pupils with English as an additional language using the DFE Proficiency Scale from levels, A to E; new to English to Fluent (DFE, 2017–18, p. 65).

What kinds of baseline scores are generated and what do they mean?

Standardised tests can generate different types of score. These might be in the form of the following:

- **An age, in years and months:** this is common for spelling and reading scores. The important thing to note here is any difference between a child's reading or spelling age and their chronological age at the time of testing.
- **A standardised score:** a standardised score is calculated in reference to an age-related national sample according to the principles outlined earlier. A standardised score of 100 represents an average performance in the test and specific numerical boundaries exist indicating low, well below and above, and well above average.
- **A raw score:** the numerical value of a raw score will vary but is a direct representation of the number of correct and incorrect responses in a specific test.
- **A percentile ranking:** it's unusual for this type of score to appear in a set of whole-school baseline data and more common in relation to diagnostic feedback. A score with a percentile ranking of 1 indicates that 99% of the age-related sample would do better in the test; the higher the percentile ranking the better the performance. 'The percentile rank of a test-taker is defined as the percentage of test-takers in the sample who gained a score at the same level or below that of the test-taker's score.'[9]

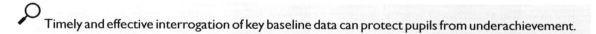

Timely and effective interrogation of key baseline data can protect pupils from underachievement.

Data should be used to inform teaching and learning.

Baseline data can refer to both measures of attainment and underlying ability.

Standardised baseline tests focus on literacy, numeracy, cognitive ability and developmental milestones.

Typical baselines include measures of reading, spelling, verbal reasoning, non-verbal reasoning and numerical reasoning.

What's involved in baseline screening?

Screening characterises a proactive approach to identifying learning difficulties and differences and can occur at key stages of pupil transition and development. The approach to identifying SEN described in the Special Educational Needs and Disability Code of Practice: 0–25 years (Code of Practice) (see Chapter 3) describes a situation where a class teacher leads on identification in response to sustained concern about pupil progress or attainment despite differentiated and High Quality Teaching.

A screening system, generally led by the SENCO or Inclusion Team, implements a comprehensive screening process that uses baseline data to identify pupils who may be experiencing learning delays or disorders and acts to support them before the impact of their needs is fully realised by low attainment and lack of progress in the curriculum. Like other types of screening, it seeks to prevent the negative impact of discernible difficulties at the earliest possible stage. Screen is therefore generally directly linked to a programme of interventions to support the development of skills or a referral system that identifies pupils who may benefit from further specialist diagnostic assessment. The school may also have access to programmes like Lucid[10] or Do-IT Profiler[11] that offer online screening tools for SpLDs like dyslexia.

Are there different considerations for screening in early years, primary and secondary schools?

This proactive approach has opportunities for both primary and secondary settings in that it offers support to teaching staff considering initial concerns about additional needs. In many ways the primary school class teacher, having more sustained relationships and greater contact with pupils and their families, can be seen to have a richer opportunity to be involved in early identification by looking at baseline data, attainment and progress expectations with the SENCO. Having worked extensively across both sectors, I find it hard to see how a Subject Specialist or Form Tutor in a secondary or even a middle school setting can develop the necessary overview quickly enough to take the lead on this process. In a secondary setting the odds are stacked against the success of a class teacher-led identification process; not least because a child meets at least a dozen new teaching staff in Year 7 and families disappear from the school gates, necessitating a more complex and coordinated system of communication.

Schools collate and present baseline data in a wide variety of ways depending on the approach they have taken to collecting and collating information, the tools they have employed to do so and the way they intend to use it.

Many providers like GL Assessments, the Centre for Evaluations and Monitoring,[12] and the National Foundation for Educational Research[13] offer highly developed, integrated online baseline reporting systems which can offer detailed, individualised feedback at pupil, group and school level. This can be used directly to provide support in terms of target settings and approaches to teaching in order to address individual needs and to identify trends.

In the absence of the kind of system described, data are often collated on the school information management system and readily available in one place via pupils and class searches. However, it is possible that as systems for baselining change over time, data on the whole cohort are inconsistent or stored in several separate files. It's important to know which scores are recorded for whom and when they were recorded. Furthermore, when looking at cognitive ability baselining it is always worth looking for the individual scores from which an average has been calculated.

Table 2.1 Collecting baseline data

Questions	Yes	No	Action/response
Is this group new to the school?			
Do I know what baseline data exist for this group?			
Do I have access to these baseline data?			
Have I looked at all of the baseline data for this group?			
Are any children missing from the information?			

Is baseline information relevant to all teachers?

The useful and exciting thing about baseline ability data is that they can reveal underlying ability and provide a key to unlock potential that has not been apparent in the classroom and that is not (yet) reflected in data on curricular progress and attainment. As a classroom teacher at any stage there are essentially two ways to use baseline data: to benchmark and thus to set targets for the pupil's performance which will allow the capturing of the improvements made from one point of measurement to the next; and to investigate patterns of ability and to understand more about the pupil and their way into learning. Some teachers may do both.

Chapter 4 refers in some depth to the advantages of forming an understanding of detailed information about the profiles of pupils with identified learning needs. If all teachers are going to be successful in teaching pupils with special education needs, some knowledge of baseline data is not only relevant but necessary.

Whether the baseline data collected relate to ability and skills in language, reading and literacy, numeracy, emotional well-being or attendance they can be a useful filter through which to view subject-specific progress and attainment. This area is plagued with vaguely off-putting acronyms such as InCAS,[14] NGRT,[15] CEM, NFER – terms that it is sometimes easier to nod along to publicly while remaining privately mystified. I would offer the reassurance that even the most complex and wordy manual can offer the layperson useful, basic information about the nature of the tests and explain the way the results are represented.

The most direct and effective way to gain insight into the experience and the demands of a test and therefore to understand the message contained in the result is to read through or even attempt the test paper yourself; comfortingly, it is likely that you will be too far beyond the age range sampled to be scored. Taking the test yourself is also useful when thinking about how results might relate directly to your teaching.

Having done this, it's important to exercise caution and be curious. Ensure that you are clear about the nature of the test and scoring system; in short, don't be guided by the numbers until you know what they mean and be especially mindful of when they were recorded. SENCOs and Inclusion Managers are generally happy to be asked about identified SEND pupils and may be able to add insights and context to details about the underlying profile of a group or an individual in detail.

Is it worth returning to baselines after the year of testing?

Looking at baselines along with progress and attainment can be informative whenever preparing to teach a new group, not just at times of major transition or when children are new to the school. As a way of checking any assumptions when preparing to teach a new group. Table 2.1 may prove useful in resetting expectations and addressing gaps in your knowledge about the pupils.

Whether the baseline is recent or historic, going back to look at underlying skills may help to refresh thinking and provide opportunities for innovation. It is possible that as the pupil progresses through school, a narrative can develop around them which emphasises certain aspects of their approach to learning while de-emphasising others. A review of baseline data can provide a refreshing contrast or context to reboot approaches to teaching and learning that have become entrenched or habitual. Going back to baselines when preparing to teach a new group can be a useful habit in that is a pertinent reminder of the pupils' starting points and challenges.

Can I use baseline data to inform subject specific teaching?

It depends on the nature of the baselining data available to you. Feedback from standardised tests of cognitive abilities tests in their simplest form provide a very different set of information to the more sophisticated online systems mentioned. Often standardised testing reveals significantly varying patterns of scores recorded across a range of ability and can therefore be extremely useful when teaching pupils whose deficit in one area is impacting their opportunity to show aptitude in another. A simple example of this would be a pupil with a low verbal score and a very high non-verbal score: without a baselining process to reveal potential it's not uncommon for the linguistic demands of the curriculum, even in mathematical or technical subjects, to have a negative impact on such a pupil's performance, subjects that should otherwise play to their strengths. It is entirely possible – indeed, it is probable – that there are pupils in your class with significant cognitive strengths who are managing significant deficits and thus looking average in terms of performance. Understanding the peaks and troughs often visible in baseline data can unlock not only empathy but release the frustration of untapped potential. Table 2.2 supports a closer look at the information available.

Schools vary in terms of the type of baseline data they collect.

It's important to be clear about the type of score that have been recorded.

Some providers report on data in narrative and diagrammatic forms that offer feedback that is highly detailed at a pupil, group and whole-school level.

It is not always easy to find baseline data that are consistent across a whole school group.

It's helpful to read or attempt test papers in order to gain insight into baseline scores.

Studying the patterns in baseline data can provide clues to unlock poor performance.

Table 2.2 Looking at baseline data

Questions	Yes	No	Action/response
Are there any pupils whose individual scores vary widely?			
Are the pupils with very low reading scores?			
Are there any low attaining pupils with high baseline scores?			
Have I cross referenced the SEND data for identified students?			
Have I cross referenced data on gifted and talented pupils?			
Are there twice-exceptional pupils in the group?			
Is there a colleague who can support me in answering my questions?			
Can I access samples of the pupils' work?			

What does the Code of Practice say about the role of baselines in making provision for pupils with SEND?

The graduated approach outlined in the Code of Practice as Assess, Plan, Do, Review requires a school to acknowledge and act on existing baseline data.

The Code clearly expects schools to establish a baseline for the skills and attainment of pupils on entry.[16] A school's procedures for baselining all of its pupils is a fundamental aspect of its duty to Assess. In doing so a school should have an identified and articulated system to collect and to collate any information related to a child's previous progress and attainment; the Code of Practice asserts this as a necessity 'in order to ensure that they build upon the pattern of learning and experience already established' (DFE, 2015, p. 95).

To enact the rest of the cycle and to Plan, Do, Review schools require points of reference, specific to their individual pupils, against which to make comparisons. The baseline is the starting point from which to measure progress.

A thorough knowledge and awareness of the range and meaning of baseline assessment tools and the data they generate offer teachers a variety of opportunities in terms of their responsibilities to employ a graduated approach:

- Individual baseline scores can provide specific measures of reading ability including accuracy and comprehension.

- Individual baseline scores can be used to identify specific areas of cognitive strength and weakness.
- Many baseline tools can be used as predictive tools against which to measure academic progress.
- Baselines tests can serve as consistent measurements, to be returned to and repeated throughout a child's education in order to chart improvements in respect to skills irrespective of changes to curriculum or curricular assessment.
- Baseline scores may implicate approaches to teaching any given pupil.
- Baseline scores may be helpful when advising pupils on curricular options.
- Baseline scores can identify patterns of performance that might indicate the need for additional diagnostic testing.

Chapter 4 deals with the last bullet point in more detail, describing the more detailed psychometric testing required to identify the specific characteristics of a SpLD. It's worth mentioning however that it is common practice for SENCOs to scrutinise baseline data. If a pupil's standardised scores differ significantly from each other, usually by 15 or more points, it is not uncommon to make a referral for further investigation.

Which baselines are relevant for pupils registered as SEN support?

Another powerful motivator for getting to grips with baseline data is the need to recognise the significant need of more than a million children in school classrooms classified as requiring and receiving SEN support.

In the year immediately following the implementation of the new Code of Practice the number of pupils identified in the single category of SEN support fell by 2.5%.[17] This fall coincided with the replacement of the previously existing categories of School Action and School Action Plus. Between January 2016 and the same month in 2017, while the percentage of pupils has remained constant at 11.6% of the pupil population, numbers of pupils recorded as SEN support have increased to 1, 002,070.

Pupils registered on school as receiving SEN support may have identified learning difficulties or SpLDs or be awaiting a diagnostic process. They do not have EHC plans and their needs may not necessarily be described in an individual plan of the type previously described. By registering a pupil in this category the school is planning to make the necessary provision to meet the pupil's educational needs within its existing resources. The support the pupil is receiving should be identified on a provision map outlining the additional or specialist resources that have been identified to do this. This support may be in the form of an 'intervention' which runs alongside or within the mainstream classroom or it could be an extra-curricular programme run by school staff or external agency. However, it is likely that a child receiving SEN support will, at least from to time, require class teaching differentiated to take account of the learning difficulties identified. In the absence of specialist reports or detailed objectives set out in an Individual Education Plan (IEP) it may be necessary to rely on close scrutiny of the existing baseline information and support from the school SENCO in order to identify underlying deficits, abilities, skills and opportunities.

Successful assessment processes logically link baselines to expectations, in order that both the curriculum and teaching is appropriate thus making targets realistic and achievable.

Surprisingly, pupils with identified SEN and even those with SpLDs may not necessarily have been through a full range of assessments. The nature of a learning difficulty can emerge over time in relation to the demands placed on the pupil. Indeed, it may be that a pupil's SEN has been only partially identified, in relation to a primary need. The graduated approach serves as an ongoing cycle for pupils receiving SEN support. Only in the light of scrutiny of a child's progress and attainment against school-wide baselines, the progress they are making in response to teaching and teaching interventions, and the data from ongoing standardised testing can this cycle operate effectively, making the identification of their SEN an ongoing process of assessment in context rather than a one off event.

The Code of Practice expects schools to establish a baseline on entry.

Baseline information offers a number of different opportunities in the successful implementation of a graduated approach.

Standardised scores that vary widely may be grounds for further testing or diagnostic assessment.

Baseline testing may reveal that a pupil with an existing learning difficulty requires further assessment and additional support.

There may be little detailed diagnostic data about pupils on SEN support.

Table 2.3 Consulting specific baseline information about SEN support pupils

Questions	Yes	No	Action/response
Have I consulted the SEND register?			
Am I aware of the identified SEN support pupils in my class?			
Have I consulted their baseline data?			
Am I aware of any specific areas of strength or specific deficits?			
Have I read the available IEP or Pupil Passports?			
Have I accessed the supporting specialist reports?			

What is different about the data available for pupils with an EHC plan?

There is always likely to be a significantly greater set of data available when a pupil has been through a process of statutory assessment that has successfully resulted in the preparation of an EHC plan (or Statement of Special Educational Needs). The information will likely be a very much more detailed variety of statistics and commentary of the type generated by the more sophisticated baseline tools and should speak to the underlying levels of ability and skills of the child identified. Depending on the nature of the learning difficulty or disability, the assessment process is likely to have comprised a number of specialist assessments of the type described in Chapter 4. The results of these specialist assessments should then form the basis of the detailed and comprehensive description of needs to be found in Section B of the EHC plan document itself. For pupils in receipt of an Education, Health and Care Plan it is arguable that the entire document constitutes baseline data and as such should be familiar to teaching staff in order to ensure that the duty expressed in the Code of Practice to 'build upon the pattern of learning and experience' (DFE, 2015, p. 94) can be honoured.

Schools will usually have systems in place, in the form of IEPs or Pupil Passport documents, to offer teaching staff a digest of essentials from the EHC plan. These supplementary documents are likely to be regularly updated and provide an overview of the current data on a pupil's strengths and weaknesses, history, points of contact for support, strategies, and resources.

In making provision to include the pupil in a mainstream setting it is logical for the teaching staff responsible for the various aspects of a child's education to have a working knowledge of the EHC plan, especially the details of the child or young person's educational needs set out in full in Section B and the special educational provision designed to meet the needs described in Section F. This strategy makes sense not least because in preparation for Annual Review it is incumbent upon staff to contribute directly to the process in terms of the extent to which pupils are working towards meeting the outcomes described in Section E. The option exists to follow best practice and to read the EHC plan in its entirety. If you are teaching a pupil with an EHC plan in a mainstream setting it is likely that the pupil will be in a small minority, limiting the impact on workload of this time-consuming activity.

Considering the huge investment of time and expertise involved in the statutory process, applying for statutory assessment, the assessment process itself and the negotiation required to arrive at an agreed final EHC plan, it seems strange that I feel the need to include a paragraph about why it should be accessible to and read by teachers.[18]

Provisos exist when the EHC plan has been in place for some time and the Local Authority has not kept the document up to date via the process of Annual Review. In such cases the supplementary planning documents produced by the school may be more accurate in reflecting the relevant changes in needs and provision. However best practice dictates that new EHC plans and updated documents should comprise the best possible overview of a child's learning difficulties, Special Educational Needs (SEN) and provision. Simply checking the date of the draft (on the last page) and making a quick comparison with the supporting documentation will reveal any significant discrepancy.

What is the structure of an Education, Health and Care plan?

The EHC plan follows the following structure (shown in Figure 2.1): The essential sections relevant to lesson planning and teaching are highlighted.

Each process that exists to filter the information contained in the needs, provision and outcomes sections of an EHC plan creates an opportunity to dilute its message and its impact.

Section	Contents
A	The views, interests and aspirations of the child and their parents, or of the young person
B	The child or young person's special educational needs
C	The child or young person's health care needs which relate to their SEN
D	The child or young person's social care needs which relate to their SEN or to a disability
E	The outcomes sought for the child or young person (including outcomes for life)
F	The special educational provision required by the child or young person
G	Any health provision reasonably required by the learning difficulties or disabilities which result in the child/YP having SEN
H1	Any social care provision which must be made for a child/YP under 18 resulting from s.2 Chronically Sick & Disabled persons Act 1970 (CSDPA
H2	Any other social care provision reasonably required by the learning difficulties or disabilities which result in the child/young person having SEN
I	Placement
J	Personal Budget (including arrangements for direct payments)
K	Advice & information

Figure 2.1 The structure of the EHC plan

In order to maintain an overview of the accuracy of the descriptions and effectiveness of the provision, teachers have to be engaged and their views considered and incorporated.

If the graduated approach enshrined in Assess, Plan, Do, Review cannot find a workable iteration within the context of an externally regulated statutory process it's hard to see how it can work effectively for pupils whose needs and progress are monitored by a school's internal systems.

The outcomes identified in the EHC plan are created and included according to the four broad areas of need identified in the Code of Practice:

*   communication and interaction;
*   cognition and learning;
*   social, emotional and mental health difficulties; and
*   sensory and/or physical needs.

Data to be considered in the case of pupils with EHC plans should include the full contents of the plan and its appendices.

Teaching staff should expect to become familiar with at least Parts B,E and F of the Plan.

Planning should link provision to the desired outcomes for the pupil – the more explicit the link the better.

Reporting on progress towards outcomes requires a consistent approach.

Planning must take into rationale, consistency and benefit to the pupil into account.

Table 2.4 Getting ready to teach pupils with EHC plans

Name of pupil			Haley Potter	
Preparation	**Yes**	**No**	**Information/action**	**Date**
Have I identified the pupils in my classes with EHC plans (or Statements)?				
Have I read the EHC plans Section B: describing learning difficulties and special educational needs?				
Have I read Section E describing outcome Section F describing provision				
Are there any specific adjustments to be made to the environment to increase access?				
Am I aware of and competent to use any assistive technology (radio-mic etc.)?				
Do I know if there will be Learning Support Assistants (LSAs) or Teaching Assistants (TAs) in any of my classes as a result of pupil with SENDs?				
Will pupils be missing from my classes to attend interventions?				
Can I relate the specific outcomes identified on EHC plan directly to my teaching this term?				
Are there identifiable next steps towards EHC objectives for pupils this term?				
Have I agreed objectives with pupils?				
Have I introduced myself to and agreed a way to communicate with pupils?				

Name of pupil			Haley Potter	
Preparation	Yes	No	Information/action	Date
Have I seen samples of pupils' work in any subjects?				
Does an understanding exist about the role of the TAs or LSAs in supporting those objectives in my classroom?				
Have I agreed on a way to communicate with the TA or SEND team to review plans?				
Have I met the support staff with whom I will work?				
How, when and to whom do I feedback on progress?				
Dates of Annual Reviews?				
Dates of ongoing diagnostic assessments?				
Date of meeting with parents/family/pupil?				

How can my familiarity with baseline data support a 'graduated approach'?

In addition to the 250,000 plus children with a Statement or an EHC plan and the 1,000,0000 plus children on SEN support there are literally countless pupils with undiagnosed learning difficulties and SpLDs whose SEN remain unspecified. Baseline data are a vital part of the identification process, described in detail in the next chapter, and as such form a consistent part of the Assess stage of the 'graduated approach'.

However, baseline data are relevant to the rest of the cycle, the Plan, Do and Review stages. It's useful to make direct links between baseline assessment data, the imminent demands of the curriculum and the process for reporting on pupils' progress.

Planning for inclusive teaching requires a significant degree of clarity, not only in accessing and interpreting *baseline* data but also in using it to link up thinking and to create a clear strategy in terms of supporting the pupil appropriately in making the often-incremental steps toward an agreed, achievable and desired *outcome*.

The success of a teacher, support assistant or programme of intervention in helping the pupil to achieve those longer-term outcomes can be aided by clarity in terms identifying incremental goals, agreeing them with pupils in the way suggested in Tables 2.1, 2.2, 2.3 and 2.4.

The provision made by the team of staff is likely to have most *impact* when there is clarity about the *baseline* and the *outcome*. In fact, this triad features so consistently in the discourse around SEN that it is tempting to arrange its elements into a neat pseudo-scientific equation.

If the graduated approach is to have integrity, then planning must be linked to a baseline and should consider either the identified outcomes as set out in the EHC plan or the targets identified in the school's planning documents.

Clearly it may be appropriate for pupils with a learning difficulty to be working towards exactly the same overarching curricular goals as their neurotypical peers, but it is likely that the journey towards at least some curricula goals will be longer and more protracted.

It is surprising how often reporting about the progress of pupils with learning difficulties becomes confusing and contradictory. An example might be a general comment about child's perceived improvement with social communication skills while later in the same report there is mention of an escalation in tension between the child and their peers in the playground. While observing variations in a pupil's behaviour is quite normal it does raise the question of what specifically is the nature of the improvement initially and if there has really been progress in terms of achievement and greater access to learning.

In working with schools consultatively, the question of how to maintain a clear overview and how to chart the progress of pupils with SEN accurately regularly arises, particularly since the demise of systems of assessment based on National Curriculum levels. Often teachers are concerned that the new assessment language of Age-Related Expectations may not offer a system that is sufficiently incremental to identify the small steps taken, in the right direction, towards longer-term goals.

While there are specific reporting tools available that address these concerns directly, they are more often used in the context of a specialist setting where each child receives the same type of detailed, incremental report. Once you have ensured that you have accessed the necessary baseline information about your identified SEND pupils, it may be useful to consider how the school reporting process can support an accurate record of their progress.

How can addressing baselines create consistency for pupils at times of transition?

Pupils with identified SEN and those going through the process of identification and diagnosis are vulnerable at time of transition. The holistic approach to baselining described in this chapter can help schools to manage transitions more effectively and ensure consistency for these vulnerable pupils: those with EHC plans, on SEN support and those with needs not yet identified.

Pupils with EHC plans should be the subject of regular meetings that prepare for and address transitions in detail, ensuring those involved in identifying, making, and monitoring provision and progress are aware of potential bumps in the road. Pupils with learning difficulties and associated SEND are particularly vulnerable at times of change for a number of different reasons. It may be that this vulnerability is exacerbated by the specific nature of the pupil's learning difficulty; pupils with autism and those with social and emotional needs may find unexpected changes of any kind to be deeply affecting and destabilizing unless carefully managed.

However, no matter the specifics of diagnosis it is important to recognise the impact of systemic inconsistency on pupils who are struggling to manage the demands of their education. It is necessary to acknowledge that the education system, and schools individually, can be hugely idiosyncratic and deeply inconsistent. School life is characterised by change – in staffing, setting, curriculum, peer group, uniform, routine and expectation. From a pupil's perspective the only common factor might be the constant and growing level of challenge that school represents.

When I work directly with children and families, they regularly describe severe anxiety around transitions large and small; even young children often recognise the differences in characteristics, approach and expectations of teachers with whom they feel they work well. They recognise that it takes time and effort on both sides to develop a working relationship – for the teachers to get to know and to understand them. Children and their families are often both mystified and exhausted by the seemingly constant need to start this process from scratch with new staff every year and, in secondary schools, multiple times over as subject teachers proliferate.

Acknowledging the workload issues central to the life of a classroom teacher, recording the details of planning for in-class provision using the format I have included can be hugely useful in creating consistency in terms of the provision around the child. If collected accurately this information can be collated and shared with new teachers or those taking over at the end of an academic year. This practice reduces the need for time-consuming handover by individual staff, avoids placing all the responsibility on the SENCO to consolidate details and generalise, or overload the Teaching Assistant (TA) who is so often relied upon as a repository of practical contextual detail.

Just as Pupil Passports work to establish a place for pupil voice in the processes of planning and review inherent in the graduated approach, the tools can be used to establish consistency for pupils and for teachers, not only in terms of identifying goals for progress and attainment but in configuring the specifics of the provision around the pupil with their involvement.

Hard lessons have been learned in the way we deal with safeguarding; statutory guidance (DFE 2015) protects children from having to repeat painful disclosures made in school and enshrines their right to be heard and have their concerns immediately addressed. SEND provision should surely adhere to the same principle. However, currently the efficacy of SEND provision relies on delegation of responsibility for the detail to an overloaded SENCO or an underqualified support teacher.

Getting to grips with baselines brings not only awareness but also clarity about what is already known and documented about a child, the details of what has worked historically, and a shared appreciation of a pupil's learning difficulties, how they emerged, and how they present.

Pupils with SEN are particularly vulnerable at times of transition.

Pupils on SEN support may need particular attention in this respect.

The value of books and folders

If we are to build on successful learning experiences and enhance a successful pattern of teaching, we need to look at all of the information related to the learning journey and attempt to consolidate key messages and implement them in the classroom.

One of the simplest ways to recognise and facilitate continuity is to make sure that books and folders containing work produced by pupils, both in class and as part of interventions, is stored or passed on to the new staff. It has been my unfortunate experience to encounter situations where an entire year's worth of work product – containing the daily record of a pupil's incremental efforts to achieve key literacy and numeracy milestones – has managed to find its way into the bin. This is the ultimate expression of a clean slate, wiped of the memories, the feedback, the celebration and struggle. Hard-won achievements are set aside, and the process is disregarded and reduced to set of average attainment grades: new year, new book, clean slate; no attempt to capture or to value the process.

Returning again to the message from the Code of Practice reminding us that establishment of and attention to baseline is designed to 'build upon the pattern of learning and experience already established' (DFE, 2015, p. 95), this speaks directly to the issues inherent in transitions. Attention to detail in terms of baseline documentation, SEND documentation and contextual data can help to mitigate some of pupil anxiety that exists around transitions by re-establishing a consensus, aiming for a consistent approach and helping to mitigate some of the limitations inherent in the structure of the current system.

Ensuring that key information about baseline, impact and outcomes is passed on both maintains and monitors the nature of provision.

Keep and value work product and incremental formative feedback.

Identify existing patterns of successful learning and build on them.

Self-evaluation

What were the key messages from this chapter?

What do I need to review?

Which activities have I tried?

Which activities would I like to try?

Things I'd like to know more about:

Is this chapter relevant to a specific situation, pupil or class?

Notes

1 More information on the uses of standardised testing can be found at the Education Endowment Foundation website: https://educationendowmentfoundation.org.uk/tools/assessing-and-monitoring-pupil-progress/testing/standardised-tests/using-standardised-tests-for-measuring-pupil-progress/

2 Details of the WRAT can be found on the Pearson Clinical website: www.pearsonclinical.co.uk/Psychology/ChildCognitionNeuropsychologyandLanguage/ChildAchievementMeasures/wrat5/wide-range-achievement-test-fifth-edition-wrat5.aspx

3 Details of the Salford Test are available on the Hodder Education website: www.hoddereducation.co.uk/New-Salford-Sentence-Reading-Test

4 Details of the NFER Group Reading test are available from the GL Assessment website: www.gl-assessment.co.uk/products/new-group-reading-test-ngrt/

5 Details of the Neale Analysis are available from the GL Assessment website: www.gl-assessment.co.uk/products/neale-analysis-of-reading-ability-nara/

6 Fred J Schonell, The Essential Spellingbook 1 – Workbook: Bk. 1 (English Skills & Practice) Paperback – 14 Jul 2000. See www.tes.com/teaching-resource/schonell-graded-spelling-test-6163797

7 Ferre Laevers (Ed.), Well-being and Involvement in Care Settings. A Process-oriented Self-evaluation Instrument, Research Centre for Experiential Education, Leuven University. ISBN: 978-90- 77343-76-8. See www.tes.com/teaching-resource/well-being-and-involvement-leuven-scale-6340990

8 Details of PASS available from GL Assessment website: www.gl-assessment.co.uk/products/pupil-attitudes-to-self-and-school-pass/

9 Nation Foundation for Education Research website: www.nfer.ac.uk/research/centre-for-assessment/standardised-scores-and-percentile-ranks/

10 Details of Lucid available from GL Assessment website: www.gl-assessment.co.uk/products/lucid/

11 Details available at Do-It Solutions Ltd website: http://doitprofiler.com/education/school/

12 Centre for Evaluation and Monitoring, University of Durham website: www.cem.org/

13 National Federation for Educational Research website: www.nfer.ac.uk/

14 Details available on InCAS from Centre for Evaluation and Monitoring, University of Durham website: www.cem.org/incas

15 Details of the NFER Group Reading test are available from the GL Assessment website: www.gl-assessment.co.uk/products/new-group-reading-test-ngrt/

16 SEND COP 2015 6.16 P 95.

17 Tania Tirraoro, Special Needs Jungle. July 2015. See www.specialneedsjungle.com/sen-figures-show-2-5-drop-in-children-with-special-educational-needs-in-england/

18 It is important that teachers or other educational professionals working closely with the child or young person should have full knowledge of the child or young person's EHC plan. 9.212 P206.

Chapter 3

How do I identify learners with SEND?

The Needs Matrix

This chapter explains the role of the teacher in identifying pupils with Special Educational Needs (SEN). It also looks at the rationale for identification of pupils set out in the Special Educational Needs and Disability Code of Practice: 0–25 years (Code of Practice).

It offers advice to the teacher about how to collect and collate the relevant information so that they may contribute effectively to the identification of a pupil with Special Educational Needs Disability (SEND).

The second part of the chapter introduces the Needs Matrix, a tool for non-specialist teachers to use to inform their observations following raising an initial concern about a pupil.

The chapter concludes by exploring the possible uses of the Needs Matrix to support a 'graduated approach' following the identification of a pupil with a learning difficulty and special educational need.

What are the responsibilities for teachers, outlined in the Code of Practice, regarding identification?

The Code of Practice outlines a key role for the class or subject teacher in making provision for pupils with SEN and in identifying them. While it does not suppose a subject specialist or class teacher to have all significant additional expertise in regard to SEN, it suggests that the process of identification should be led by them and supported by the SENCO.

 'In identifying a child as needing SEN support the class or subject teacher, working with the SENCO, should carry out a clear analysis of the pupil's needs.'

(DFE, 2015, p. 100)

In a few short words the Code of Practice places a significant responsibility on the classroom teacher to recognise and to meet needs. Even the most experienced classroom practitioner could be forgiven for feeling somewhat overwhelmed by this responsibility as it is one for which teacher training has historically made little preparation. The Code makes several assumptions in delegating this responsibility, principally that the teacher in question has access to the necessary information, the specialist knowledge and skills to be able to interpret the information and the opportunity within the school's structures and scheduling to co-ordinate their efforts and manage the workload.

What's the role of the teacher in terms of the responsibilities outlined by the school?

The specifics of the teacher's role should be explicit in the school's SEN Policy or SEN Information report. The specifics are likely to depend on the type of school; mainstream, special, alternative, the phase of teaching and the articulated rationale for the identification process. Whether or not the classroom teacher is to lead on identification or work according to the direction of other colleagues, active participation in the process is a common expectation in almost all educational settings and in the best interest of all concerned, not least the pupil.

In terms of the responsibilities outlined in the Code of Practice, what is the role of the SENCO in identifying a pupil with SEN?

Support for teachers in addressing SEND should come in the form of 'professional guidance' from the SENCO. However, the Code of Practice is careful not to suggest that the SENCO has any exclusive responsibility to identify of a pupil's SEN. In respect of supporting colleagues in making the provision outlined in the graduated approach, the SENCO role is characterised in terms of strategy, oversight, guidance and co-ordination (DFE, 2015, p. 108).

It is relevant to note that in this important respect the description of the SENCO role in the Code of Practice is heavy on liaison and facilitation and light on specialist knowledge. The Code does not suggest that specialist advice and support for classroom teachers is readily available in schools.

Again, the specifics of the SENCO or Inclusion Manager's role should be explicit in the school's SEN Policy or SEN Information report. The SENCO must be named in the document and their contact details provided.

It may be that the school shares a SENCO with other schools and has subsumed the role into that of a deputy or has a large department with more than one SENCO acting for different cohorts. In any event it is always a good idea to identify the SENCO and familiarise yourself with points of contact and any schedule for advice, support and training. As the member of staff charged with the 'day-to-day responsibility for the operation of SEN policy' (DFE, 2015, p. 108) they are the 'go to' source of information for questions regarding the school's approach.

What is the rationale for making an identification according to the Code of Practice?

Schools are expected to have systems of identification in place that acknowledge and identify learning difficulties and related SEN. If there is evidence that a pupil might have a disability schools have a duty under the Equality Act 2010 to make reasonable adjustments for them.

The Code of Practice describes a number of circumstances which might lead a teacher to initiate a process of identification; it offers a set of considerations or stimuli. It does not offer a set of instructions or a specific structure for the identification process. While covering all bases, in terms of noting the potential sources of assessment data and contextual information on pupil performance and ability, the Code does little to describe a clear rationale in terms of where, when or how to start.

While a cornerstone of identification tends to be levels of progress and attainment that fall below age-related norms, schools are expected to be able to distinguish a learning delay due to temporary or circumstantial reason from a learning disorder requiring specific diagnosis and intervention.

'Where progress continues to be less than expected the class or subject teacher, working with the SENCO, should assess whether the child has SEN.'

(DFE, 2015, p. 94)

Suggested considerations for the process of identification include:

- slow or slowing progress rates and attainment gaps as key indicators of SEN;
- the impact of targeted, high quality, differentiated teaching as a first response to slow or slowing progress rates and attainment gaps;
- the pupil's response to extra teaching and interventions which may contribute to identifying their particular needs and/or improve progress and attainment;
- the desired outcome;
- sustained concern in respect of progress and attainment;
- the fact that age-appropriate attainment does not preclude the occurrence of learning difficulty or disability; and
- all data available, including progress, attainment, age-related expectations, formative assessment, views of pupil and family, and information from specialist and external agencies 'for higher levels of need'.

The repeated references to underachievement, slow progress, attainment gaps and failure strongly suggests that the principal driver for assessment and identification of SEN is incidence of underachievement. While the Code of Practice nods to the fact that some children with age-appropriate attainment may also have a special educational need, it goes no further in terms of advising teachers on what else to monitor or how to do it.

It's hard to argue against the logic of having a system in place to address the needs of pupils whose progress and attainment is lower or slower than most of their peers. However, it is important to note that while this is an important criterion, there are exceptions. Meeting some of all of the age-related norms academically does not preclude a pupil from experiencing a learning difficulty or requiring a special provision to meet an educational need.

Meeting age-related norms does not preclude a child from experiencing a learning difficulty.

What is the role of pre-emptive support before identification of a learning difficulty?

When I trained in the 1990s it was a widely accepted rule of thumb that in order for a pupil to access the Key Stage 3 curriculum independently they would require a Reading Age of at least 10 years and 6 months. It sounds obvious now that the curriculum for an 11-year-old requires the commensurate reading ability but the impact of taking this simple baseline measure and acting on it pre-emptively in advance of the first full curricula reporting cycle was powerful. Identifying pupils whose skills in reading fell below this ceiling and offering them targeted and sustained support designed to get them to it afforded several opportunities, namely, the opportunity to work more closely with pupils to:

- identify the specific gaps in their knowledge;
- focus teaching;
- closely observe and monitor progress;
- moderate the demands of the curriculum;
- build self-esteem by recognising incremental progress;
- to distinguish between pupils with a learning delay and learning difficulty or disability likely to have a longer-term impact; and
- to monitor, observe and create a database on which to judge the need for further diagnostics assessment.

What is the rationale for the identification of SEN outlined by the school?

The SEN Information Report should explain the school's rationale for the identification of pupils and place it within the context of a guide to the school's SEN provision as a whole. Most importantly, for teachers, it should detail key responsibilities, systems and processes for staff to use. It should also set out the nature and arrangements for access to any specialist provision, resources or expertise. Remembering that there may be a degree of specialism or variation in almost all respects described in the list that follows, it is necessary for class teachers to become familiar with the document in order for the system to work and for policy to inform practice and vice versa.

The SEN information report[1] should contain the following

- the kinds of SEN that are provided for at school (name and contact for SENCO);
- policies (practices) for identifying;
- arrangements for consulting parents;
- arrangements for consulting young people;
- arrangements for assessing and reviewing progress;
- arrangements for supporting movement between phases of education;
- the approach to teaching;
- how adaptations are made to the curriculum and learning environment;
- how the curriculum is made accessible;
- the expertise and training of staff;
- how specialist expertise is secured and funded;
- evaluating the effectiveness of the provision (its impact);
- how children and young people with SEN are enabled to engage in all activities;
- nature of support for improving emotional and social development (pastoral arrangements);
- how the school involves external agencies and services (Local Authority);
- arrangements for handling complaints about the provision;
- arrangements for supporting SEN pupils who are looked after;
- clear, straightforward language of information; and
- named school contact for pupils and parents with concerns.

How does a class teacher 'assess whether a pupil has Special Educational Needs' and lead on an 'analysis' of those needs?

There is something of the chicken and the egg about the way the Code of Practice refers to identification. It's worth thinking about the language used to describe the processes of assessment that comprises this 'identification'. In the Code the focus of the assessment to be carried out by the teacher is the child's 'educational needs'. The learning difficulty or difficulties are not mentioned explicitly but subsumed into the child's resulting needs. This can be an unhelpful and misleading shorthand for the teacher charged with identification. Technically an identification of SEN is dependent on the occurrence of learning difficulty or disability. Therefore, logic suggests (as does the process of statutory assessment) that the foundation of an any assessment of Special Educational Needs (SEN) is an assessment of learning difficulties or disabilities. The Code seems to imply that these two processes are one and the same. However, difficulties and disabilities are not the same as SEN. Imagine a pupil with a dyslexic-type pattern of difficulties; let's say these include poor auditory memory, weak phonological awareness and slow processing speeds. Let's also say that as a result the pupil has a severely depressed reading age. The nature of this learning difficulty is a constant across the curriculum; however, the nature of the demands placed on the pupil in various lessons from English, PE, Art, Design Technology and French changes and re-characterises the nature not of the difficulty but of the resultant educational need. In PE lessons the pupil may require instructions to be repeated or modelled; in English lessons the pupil may require a laptop with read-out-loud software; in French lessons they may require a slower pace to the introduction of new vocabulary and supplementary visual stimulus to aid memory. To provide an 'analysis' of a pupil's special educational need the teacher has to understand the nature, scope and impact of the difficulty in educational context. It's therefore logical to assume that before a teacher and a SENCO can analyse the child's needs they first need to investigate and describe the nature of the difficulties and their likely impact on school based learning. If schools are to accurately be able to describe the provision necessary to meet a child's SEN, there has to be a holistic and forensic approach to identifying learning difficulties and their impact on pupil performance across the full breadth of the curriculum.

How does a teacher contribute to the identification of a learning difficulty, disorder or disability?

The only practical way to approach this considerable challenge is to make provision to optimise the ability of a class teacher to take the lead on recognition and referral, to participate in the collection of reliable information about the pupil in a useful format.

The process of identification begins with a teacher's acknowledgement of something distinct and unusual in the way a pupil is responding to teaching or an acknowledgement that a pupil is somehow struggling to cope with one or more aspects of the standard school experience.

The Code of Practice allows for progress and attainment to be addressed in a targeted way before any formal processes of SEN assessment get underway, therefore a pupil's response to any directed, differentiated, additional or support teaching can provide a useful additional insight to the process. Identification works best when teachers create opportunities to view progress and attainment in the broadest possible broader context. The Needs Matrix helps to structure and direct this.

If teachers are to fully acknowledge the range and scope of all of the four categories of need, observations and information should refer to each aspect: learning and cognition, social communication and language, emotional health, and sensory or physical well-being and development.

Identification of a learning difficulty and resulting SEN requires a forensic approach to information gathering.

The Needs Matrix can be used to inform and assist the process of identification.

The Needs Matrix can be used in a variety of ways, after identification, to support evidence-based discussion about a pupil's difficulties, learning and progress.

Using the Needs Matrix to support identification of pupils with learning difficulties and SEN

What is the Needs Matrix?

The Needs Matrix is a prompt to classroom observations; it is a tool with which to collect and collate notes on learning behaviour and habits in context and in conjunction with work produced. From the outset when registering a concern, even informally, it's important for the teacher to recognise that forming a hypothesis is much less important than collecting evidence. The Needs Matrix is designed to help classroom teachers look beyond the progress and attainment data and the demands-specific curricular demands of their subject and to shift focus on to the learning behaviour and habits of the pupil: their underlying abilities to manage independent learning successfully. The Needs Matrix is not a tool concerned with labelling a pupil but with recognising the impact of a potentially undiagnosed need.

Essentially, the Needs Matrix is a checklist of concerns that may help a teacher to better focus and target High Quality Teaching. It does so by inviting the teacher to consider the pupil's performance in classwork and homework according to a comprehensive list of traits common to the most prevalent SpLDs and disorders. In doing so it is possible to consider opportunities to address the difficulties observed and to keep track of the response.

How does the Needs Matrix differ from conventional checklists for SpLD?

While many individual checklists exist to support the identification of SpLDs like Dyslexia Dyspraxia (DCD) or ADHD it's clear from the evidence about co-morbidity (discussed in Chapter 4) that children are less likely to present with a set of needs that conform rigidly to one diagnosis. SpLDs may also co-occur with autism. Diagnoses of SpLDs are rarely straightforward, often combining a unique list of traits that occur across a range of diagnoses. The Needs Matrix therefore brings together in one document descriptors from all of the most prevalent SpLDs, referring to each of the four categories of need as described in the Code of Practice.

What are the advantages of using the Needs Matrix?

Using the Needs Matrix as part of a process of identification and analysis of a child's SpLDs and SEN may help to identify specific features of a pupil's approach to learning in the light of concern.

The Needs Matrix encourages teachers to focus on the specifics of a pupil's performance at school. It invites teachers to rate the occurrence and frequency of a number of features of learning associated with a variety of common SpLDs. The Matrix offers the teacher an aide memoire about features of common SpLDs. This can support the development of knowledge and skills pertinent to assessing whether or not a pupil has a learning difficulty and conducting an analysis of Special Educational Need.

To lead an evidence-based discussion with parents

This can help enormously in supporting evidence-based discussions with parents, colleagues and outside agencies. It also helps us to avoid the perils of anecdotal third-party record keeping – which often tells us more about the writer than it does the child. The Needs Matrix enables a discussion informed by fact, breadth and overview, not subjectivity or conjecture.

To provide specific feedback to SENCOs

Teachers are often expected to contribute to processes of assessment summatively or retrospectively. When SENCOs are compiling evidence for referrals, and especially when initiating or progressing processes of statutory assessment, they have a responsibility to detail the provision made by the school to that point. Information from a completed Needs Matrix can capture both the process of identification and the attempts at making provision to meet needs. The Matrix can be a helpful tool to evidence action taken by the classroom teacher from the outset and as such provide evidence that a child's needs are genuinely different from and additional to that which is available.

In supporting referral to a specialist external agency

While it's clear that relevant and consistent diagnostic expertise is not automatically available across all phases and settings (all diagnostic and therapeutic specialist services appear to be highly pressured and in short supply) it becomes even more important to ensure that this limited resource is directed appropriately. The Needs Matrix can help you to contribute useful, objective information not just on progress and attainment but on a child's approach to learning in school, in all its variety.

To track the impact of support strategies including use of LSAs and TAs

The Matrix is not the preserve of the classroom teacher. It can be used to direct the TA or Learning Support Assistant (LSA) to observe, support or monitor specific aspects of a pupil's learning or can be used by the LSA to direct and record their intervention.

To compare learning behaviours across a range of settings: subject, time of day, location, group etc.

To be most effective the analysis should take place across the curriculum and indeed in extra-curricular, unstructured and home environments. It's essential to recognise that a pupil's learning difficulty may well reveal itself in different ways in different areas of the curriculum. Only by looking across a range of learning experiences does a more complete picture emerge, allowing for areas of strength and ability to come to the fore alongside areas of concern. Therefore, it is possible to configure the collection of information in many different ways. The Needs Matrix can be used by a single member of staff in different lessons and situations including breaks and extra-curricular settings; it can be repeated at regular intervals or can be completed by different staff simultaneously or in different settings. The data from a number of forms from can be compared and collated to ensure that judgements are made based on objective and comprehensive information.

The solutions to more effective differentiation, targeted support or pupil motivation may already exist in other areas of the curriculum.

To map progress regarding a specific target area

The Needs Matrix can be adapted, and the traits listed reduced, to target specific areas of concern around which to focus planning or to collect information about progress and attainment.

To reinforce knowledge and encourage the use of appropriate terminology

Use of the Needs Matrix allows teachers to become familiar with the relevant, common terminology used to describe SpLDs. It also reinforces knowledge and understanding of the characteristics of a number of SpLDs.

To address multiple and complex needs

The list of traits is not exhaustive. The Needs Matrix can be augmented and personalised to reflect concerns as they emerge.

To structure monitoring and replace anecdotal reporting

Considering the significant expectations on schools to produce reliable and detailed historic data regarding SEN provision, especially in relation to processes of referral and statutory assessment, records have a tendency to be idiosyncratic and anecdotal. They are often time-consuming to produce and subjective in terms of content. The Needs Matrix allows the teacher to identify the areas concern, action and monitoring, thus creating a structure for feedback.

To inform planning, to retain and share good practice

The information contained in the Needs Matrix can easily be collated, compared and shared with colleagues. The Needs Matrix Action Plan can be used to develop, record and share a strategy for targeted support and in this way, explicitly map the link between differentiated, high quality teaching and pupil need.

To triangulate performance, classroom support and educational needs

Its hugely difficult to establish a causal link between supported and differentiated classroom teaching and pupil progress in relation to an identified difficulty and educational need. Other than regarding specific programmes of intervention that focus teaching on moving a single baseline score – e.g. participation in a paired reading scheme it's almost impossible to quantify impact. The Matrix creates an opportunity to collect detailed information about a pupil's response to targeted classroom teaching and support. In this way a matrix can act as a snapshots of impact over time.

Why is the Needs Matrix in an adaptable format?

The Needs Matrix Form is available as a Microsoft Word file rather than a PDF, making it easier to adapt as you move forward – discarding and embellishing traits as they emerge or are discounted.

How does the Needs Matrix save time?

The Needs Matrix (shown in Table 3.1) is designed to acknowledge that workload issues and time management are possibly the greatest challenge faced by teachers. The Matrix assists in that it helps to avoids the need to record information on planning and provision for SEN in the form of a lengthy written narrative, it can be completed quickly but provides highly specific feedback.

Table 3.1 Needs Matrix

		Please tick*			Comments
Current attainment in your subject		**B**	**E**	**A**	
Rate behaviours affecting learning adversely – there is no need to rate every descriptor		**Frequency rating**			
		High	**Medium**	**Low**	
1	Keeping things in mind				
2	Remembering processes/sequences				
3	Remembering images and symbols				
4	Plan and do (completing written tasks)				
5	Processing sounds				
6	Remembering sounds				
7	Matching phoneme to grapheme				

(Continued)

Table 3.1 (Continued)

		Please tick*			Comments
Current attainment in your subject		**B**	**E**	**A**	
Rate behaviours affecting learning adversely – there is no need to rate every descriptor		**Frequency rating**			
		High	**Medium**	**Low**	
8	Slow pace				
9	Reading – speed/fluency/comprehension				
10	Spelling				
9	Laterality (right from left)				
10	Core stability				
11	Fine and gross motor skills				
12	Proprioception (awareness of body in space)				
13	Co-ordination				
14	Balance				
15	Concepts of number				
16	Algebra				

	Please tick*			Comments
Current attainment in your subject	**B**	**E**	**A**	
Rate behaviours affecting learning adversely – there is no need to rate every descriptor	**Frequency rating**			
	High	**Medium**	**Low**	
17	Complex calculations			
18	Proximity			
19	Relating to peers			
20	Playing			
21	Conversations			
22	Appropriate responses			
23	Awareness of social cues			
24	Range of interests			
25	Eye contact			
26	Social understanding and interaction			
27	Non-verbal and verbal communication			
28	Imagination and flexible thinking			

(Continued)

Table 3.1 (Continued)

	Please tick*			Comments
Current attainment in your subject	**B**	**E**	**A**	
Rate behaviours affecting learning adversely – there is no need to rate every descriptor	**Frequency rating**			
	High	**Medium**	**Low**	
29	Blurting				
30	Turn taking				
31	Lack of participation				
32	Fidgety				
33	Day dreaming				
34	Focus				
35	Reluctance to switch activities				
36	Difficulty sitting				
37	Constant fidgeting				
38	Out of seat				
39	Taps and drums				
40	Dislikes getting dirty hands				

		Please tick*			Comments
Current attainment in your subject		**B**	**E**	**A**	
Rate behaviours affecting learning adversely – there is no need to rate every descriptor		**Frequency rating**			
		High	**Medium**	**Low**	
41	Throws very hard				
42	Breaks pencil when writing				
43	Verbal comprehension				
44	Expressive language				
45	Pragmatics				
46	Semantics				
47	Articulation				

What do I do with the feedback collected using the Needs Matrix?

Once you have used the Needs Matrix to identify areas of concern either independently or in co-operation with colleagues, it's necessary to review the information and possibly create a digest reconciling the feedback so far. This can be done by simply tallying the frequency ratings for each descriptor and identifying priority areas or concerns across the curriculum. It may be useful to think through an action plan as first response and look at how teaching can target any of the identified areas.

The Needs Matrix Action Plan in Table 3.2 includes only areas of difficulty that have arisen at high frequency across the curriculum. The teacher has considered a plan using the suggestions for effective differentiation (DR GOPTA) in Chapter 6 to identify a plan for targeted teaching and support. This format can then be used to monitor progress.

Table 3.2 Needs Matrix Action Plan

Number	Difficulty	Strategy (DR GOPTA)		Cross curricular goal
5	Processing sounds	Ability to recognise syllables in words and to clearly articulate most common two-syllable words	1.	To clearly articulate and to repeat and to provide visual cues for key two-syllable words, to model and to invite repetition
			2.	To work with Group X in literacy sessions
			3.	To ensure that new words are highlighted in colour for ease of support at home
			4.	LSA to check cumulative word list over a six-week period and identify progress and gaps
7	Matching phoneme to grapheme	To recognise and to reproduce *spr, scr, str, shr*, initial triple blends correctly	1.	To provide visual cue for blends, tabs for reading books, sticky notes and cue cards
			2.	To model and to practice pronunciation with LSA
			3.	To link to tasks across curriculum
			4.	Invite pupil to choose next blends from phonics checklist
			5.	To provide frequent feedback on successes
			6.	Modify and specify spelling expectations to encourage mastery approach
9	Reading: speed/ fluency/ comprehension	To increase accuracy and comprehension of age-appropriate material	1.	Identify and select appropriate and engaging reading material – fiction and non-fiction
			2.	Paired reading daily at home/peer mentor/ LSA
			3.	Miscue analysis twice each half term

Number	Difficulty	Strategy (DR GOPTA)	Cross curricular goal	
12	Proprioception (awareness of body in space)	Reduction in knocks and trips when negotiating classroom environment	1.	Practise transitions in empty classroom
			2.	Review arrangement of class furniture
			3.	Establish equipment routine
37	Constant fidgeting	Increased focus and work product	1.	Observe behaviour
			2.	Offer appropriate manipulative and time manage
			3.	Instigate controlled learning breaks in form of duties involving movement
			4.	Reduce clutter and increase working space in group

Can the Needs Matrix be used to supplement information about a pupil already identified?

In the course of the graduated approach, Assess is part of a cycle rather than a one-off event. The Needs Matrix can be used to provide detail concerning an initial referral or indeed to acknowledge an emerging concern or to collect information about an area of difficulty not yet fully investigated.

It is entirely possible for a pupil with identified learning difficulties to have undiagnosed and unrecognised associated difficulties; even in cases where a statutory assessment has resulted in an Education, Health and Care plan it is possible for additional needs to emerge at different times and in response to different stimuli.

It's important to cross reference the existing SEND register, baseline and attainment data and to consider what is already known and documented. There may be specialist reports, Individual Learning Plans (ILPs) or Pupil Passports available for some children that can quickly answer queries and concerns. However, it may be that a provision made previously was prematurely curtailed by a change in circumstance and that a change of school or location and that a new referral of some kind is required.

Note

1 Full list to be found on P106 and 107 of the Code of Practice 2015, DFE.

Self-evaluation

What were the key messages from this chapter?

What do I need to review?

Which activities have I tried?

Which activities would I like to try?

Things I'd like to know more about:

Is this chapter relevant to a specific situation, pupil or class?

Chapter 4

What are 'core deficits'?

In explaining the way intelligence is traditionally assessed and described, by the measurement of memory and processing, this chapter identifies deficits common to many SpLDs. It looks at the impact of these common deficits on the core activities of teaching and learning.

The typical features of an Educational Psychologist's report are translated, and the reader is offered an understanding of the underlying cognitive issues.

The chapter goes on to make links between the deficits, classroom performance and teaching strategies to provide the reader with a template for action, monitoring and review of individual needs.

What do I know about intelligence?

Following the innovation of neuroimaging at the beginning of this century, the dynamic and exciting impact of cognitive neuroscience has added greatly to the discourse around SpLDs. Dyslexia has been repeatedly identified as a neurological rather than psychological condition. However, this distinction is difficult to make in an educational context where SpLDs are predominantly diagnosed by Educational Psychologists (EPs) using a variety of psychometric tests and measures of attainment.

Considering that a teacher's stock in trade is the development of their pupil's knowledge and skills, surprisingly little teacher training time is spent talking about the concept of intelligence – how it has been constructed over time, how it is measured and how those measurements are expressed. Special Educational Needs (SEN) and SpLDs are much better understood in the light of this knowledge.

Intelligence is an abstract concept referring to a person's ability to acquire knowledge and apply skills; however, unlike other abstractions such as empathy or creativity it is something scientists have sought to measure and to quantify using a variety of assessments generally referred to as 'psychometric tests'.

The notion of an intelligence quotient (IQ), a score defining intellectual ability, developed during the late 19th and early 20th centuries. The Simon-Binet Test, first published in 1905, was a test predominantly of verbal ability devised in order to distinguish intellectual ability from mental illness in children. Non-verbal tests became more common after the USA developed and implemented tests of mental aptitude to select army recruits and assign them appropriate duties in the First World War. The widely used Wechsler Intelligence Scale for Children, now in its fifth version,[1] was first introduced in 1949 and comprises more than 10 different subtests, reflecting its author David Wechsler's belief that intelligence comprises a number of specific but interrelated functions. The debate, ongoing today, about the multifaceted nature of intellectual ability and the need to measure both quantitively and qualitatively reaches back through the origins and development of testing.

While most of us are familiar with the concept of an IQ, test only a small percentage of us have actually completed a full-scale IQ test. Understanding how the test works and how it is administered is invaluable when working to implement the recommendations for the child for whom a report has been produced.

In 2017 the configuration of a full-scale IQ comprises a number of tests and can take about three hours to complete. It is usually administered on a one-to-one basis by an EP. The test comprises two main types of measure: verbal (verbal comprehension and working memory); performance (perceptual organization and processing speed). The EP will also consider, observe and comment on the child's history, behaviour, approach and attitude during testing.

Intelligence refers to a person's ability to acquire knowledge and skills.

The concept of intelligence and an IQ has evolved over time.

Intelligence is multifaceted.

Measures of intelligence are complex and employ many subtests to explore verbal and performance abilities.

What is a specific learning difficulty?

A child with a SpLD experiences difficulties with specific, identifiable aspects of learning and processing; these specific difficulties occur across the range of intellectual ability, with varied severity and impact.

SpLDs affect the way information is learned and processed. They are neurological (rather than psychological), usually run in families and occur independently of intelligence. They can have significant impact on education and learning and on the acquisition of literacy skills.'[2]

The most commonly occurring SpLDs are dyslexia, dyspraxia, ADD, ADHD and dyscalculia. These SpLDs may also occur in the context of autism. SpLDs are often contrasted with general or global learning difficulties indicated by low levels of performance across a range of measures of ability. It's thought that SpLDs affect between 4% and 10% of the UK population with varying degrees of severity.

It's likely that an SpLD will have a negative impact on a child's acquisition of literacy and or numeracy while also affecting some, or all, of the following;

- time management;
- memory;
- organization;
- visual processing;
- auditory processing;
- sensory sensitivity;
- distractibility; and
- visual stress.

A SpLD can be described in detail following the production of a report from an Educational Psychologist (EP) and/or other specialist practitioner.

Dyslexia is often described by EPs as a specific pattern of cognitive difficulties. This pattern is created by a wide-ranging performance in tests of memory and cognition, indicating areas of above average, average and below average ability. Plotted on a graph, a characteristically 'spikey profile' of peaks and troughs emerge.

Dyspraxia, otherwise known as Developmental Co-ordination Disorder (DCD), affects a child's physical co-ordination in terms of their fine and/or gross motor skills and co-ordination, causing them to perform less well than expected in daily activities. Diagnosis will usually involve referral to and an assessment by an Occupational Therapist.

ADD and ADHD are neurological conditions impacting a child's ability to maintain attention and focus. ADHD indicates that the child's inattention is combined with a heightened need for stimulus and activity. It's possible the route to diagnosis may be via a learning disability specialist practitioner or via a GP to a child psychiatrist.

Dyscalculia is characterised by difficulties in learning mathematical facts, numerical magnitude and other fundamentals that may include concepts of number, counting, measuring, calculating and orientation. Dyscalculia is identified by specialist teachers or EPs based on the interpretation of a range of measures.

Language disorder is the revised term describing children with 'language difficulties that create obstacles to communication or learning in everyday life and is associated with poor prognosis. Developmental Language Disorder was the agreed term for when the language disorder is not associated with a known condition' (Royal College of Speech and Language Therapists, 2018). Both are identified following assessment by a Speech and Language Therapist or pathologist and affect specific aspects of language processing and communication in the absence of physiological and developmental delay.

An EP identifies SpLD following testing and in relation to specific patterns of ability.

SpLDs can occur across the full range of intellectual ability.

A SpLD affects more than reading and writing.

There are many SpLDs including dyslexia, ADD and dyspraxia.

What is meant by 'core deficits'?

Following assessment, it's likely that diagnostic testing has revealed several underlying problems. These may be areas of poor functioning in terms of memory and processing that often serve to undermine the development of skills necessary for independent learning identified earlier. There are several deficits that commonly feature in the diagnosis of several, different, SpLDs.

Finding ways to acknowledge these underlying deficits and their impact on the core business of independent learning can offer insights to teachers struggling to support pupils. Three commonly occurring deficits affecting core activities for independent learning include the following.

> **Poor working memory** indicates the pupil has a reduced capacity to store information that is temporarily required for processing and can impact the processing of both verbal and visual information. Working memory is distinct from short-term memory in that it relates to the ability to work with information rather than simply remember it for a short time. In Ross and Tracy Alloways' book, *The Working Memory Advantage*, it is characterized as the brain's 'conductor' that serves to: 'prioritise and process' and 'to hold onto information' (Alloway & Alloway, 2013) in order to work with it. They also explain the importance of working memory as a reliable predictor of educational success and describe its impact on daily life.
>
> **Slow processing time** means pupils with learning difficulties often take significantly longer than their peers to think about information and to process stimuli. This affects a pupil's performance irrespective of their capacity to understand, remember or use information.
>
> **Phonological processingdifficulties** directly affect the processing of speech sounds. Difficulties may occur in a number of respects: awareness of the sound structure of language; ability to retrieve sounds and associate them with letters; and the ability to store and retrieve sounds from working memory. Difficulties with one or more of these aspects clearly has direct impact on literacy development.

Commonly occurring difficulties underlying SpLDs include poor working memory, slow processing time and phonological processing difficulties.

These difficulties impact the development of knowledge and skills that form a core requirement for independent and school-based learning.

What is co-morbidity?

For some time, studies have strongly suggested that specific difficulties are less likely to occur alone and more likely to present with at least one co-morbid disorder. For example, some studies have shown up to 70% overlap between dyslexic and dyspraxic groups (O'Hare & Khalid, 2002). To appreciate fully the scope and impact of a child's strengths and weaknesses a '360 approach' is most likely to provide a more complete picture of the specific difficulties or disorders that give rise to SEN. Therefore, it may well be necessary for assessments to be carried out by an EP, a Speech and Language Therapist, and an Occupational Therapist.

Given the facts about co-morbidity, it is worth noting that the process of sorting and recording pupils in a single specific category, derived from the categories in the Special Educational Needs and Disability Code of Practice: 0–25 years (Code of Practice), is likely to represent an oversimplification and a best-fit judgement about 'primary' need.

This means that full and accurate data about the actual occurrence of specific difficulties in whole school populations is largely unavailable.

- Communication and interaction
- Cognition and learning
- Social, mental and emotional
- Sensory and or physical

 SpLDs often occur in combination.

Can specialist diagnostic information inform classroom practice?

Bearing in mind the fact that as of July 2017 just over 14% of the total pupil population have an identified special educational need, it is highly likely that most, if not all, classes include at least one child with one or more SpLDs. In mainstream primary schools and mixed ability secondary classrooms it is likely that several children will be affected, and a range of SpLDs could be in evidence.

It's entirely possible that, as a classroom teacher, you won't have had the opportunity to read a full diagnostic report from a specialist practitioner (EP, Speech and Language Therapist or Occupational Therapist etc.). This may be due to a school system that exists to filter such information. It may be that the school SENCO has produced an Individual Education Plan (IEP) or Pupil Passport document to assist you in your planning and that it contains material from the report or reports in digest form. While it can be extremely helpful to understand the current strategy for support and the details of provision likely contained in such a document, there are many good reasons to access and read a full report because a greater depth of knowledge may well be necessary in certain circumstances:

- if you are the primary class teacher and have responsibility for a child's progress and attainment for a whole year;
- if you are a pastoral point of contact (mentor or form tutor) in secondary school; and
- if you are finding it difficult to manage the needs of the pupil in the classroom.

Whether you are looking for ways to make an existing provision work, to differentiate teaching or prepare for a conversation with the pupil and their family about transition or aspirations there is a tacit understanding that school 'knows' what has been previously documented. Pupils and families expect teachers to be able to recognise the apparent and the underlying issues with their child's learning difficulties.

Given the investment of time, effort and money made by everyone involved in the production of a diagnostic assessment, not least by the child, it is surprising to recognise the relatively limited audience they receive. Often remaining the preserve of the SENCO or Inclusion Manager alone. The child and family concerned are like to have had a challenging time in school, and have certainly participated in a lengthy and challenging assessment process. It's hard to see how a school and its governors can be using their 'best endeavours' to make appropriate provision for children with Special Educational Needs Disability (SEND) if key teaching staff are not expected to engage directly with a rich seam of advice and information often filed away on a hard drive or kept in a locked cabinet.

On a practical note, it's important to be mindful of the fact that the reports contain personal and sensitive information; there is a very real need to be clear about the need to respect confidentiality and be aware of data protection responsibilities. In terms of access, it may be that hard copies of reports are rarely distributed but may be found in a protected area of the school server or in the relevant administrative space or SENCO office. If you are accessing a report online it's important to think carefully about the environment in which the contents should be viewed.

It is also important to note the date of the report and to consider whether there may be amended or updates documents on file. Schools tend to have a 'keep everything' attitude to filing, so a few additional minutes invested in picking through documents to find the most current version might save time in the long run.

What's to be gained from this investment of time?

- It provides a detailed set of baselines and can illustrate the underlying cognitive and processing difficulties (core deficits) that explain a child's struggle to learn.
- It can offer insight to the subject specialist, enabling direct connections to be made between areas of difficulty and the specific demands of the curriculum area.
- It can identify areas of relative strength and ability.
- It often includes suggestions in terms of materials, tools and approaches to learning.
- It provides important information about a pupil's history of difficulties, how they emerged, and the family's perspective and journey.
- There is also much to be gained in terms of continued professional development in terms of understanding the diagnostic process itself and the nature of SpLDs.

It's vital to access the existing information about a child's learning profile and become aware of the nature of their difficulties.

It can be very useful to look at data about baselines and attainment in the light of diagnostic information.

How are specialists' reports structured?

Referral and background: This section will include information from home and school about reasons for referral in the form of current concerns and a developmental history from home and of previous education and any current provision.

Appearance and behavioural observations: This section will record details of the subject's behaviour at the assessment itself; including how they present emotionally and physically, and a summary of any discussion.

Test results: This section will provide details and most likely a brief description of every test administered, and the results produced. The results are likely to be presented both in narrative prose and tabulated form. It's likely that an EP will perform more than one type of testing depending on the range of concerns (e.g. cognitive, attainment, phonological processing and handwriting).

Summary and conclusions: This section will offer an overview, potentially identifying a diagnosis or diagnoses. It may include relevant information from previous specialist reports. It will also provide a tabulated summary of all of the test results.

Recommendations: This section may include advice on further assessment and therapeutic support required from psychiatry, clinical or educational psychology, Occupational Therapy or Speech and Language therapy. It may include advice to parents on managing difficulties at home and how to manage sharing a diagnosis. The recommendations should also contain detailed advice on specialist and classroom teaching strategies, including advice on resources and adaptations and any special provisions for examinations.

Appendices: This section will contain more detailed explanations of the structure and process of evaluation specific to each separate test administered.

Whether you are dealing with one specialist report or more, with or without additional information from an ILP, IEP or Pupil Passport it's likely that planning will require the collation and consolidation of information.

Specialist reports follow a prescribed format and include information relevant to classroom teaching.

How do I record important diagnostic information and keep things in mind?

As it is possible that there may be more than one type of diagnostic report available and that each report is densely packed with information there is a pressing need to prioritise and to find a way to distil the important messages and get the gist of a complex set of information.

The format shown in Table 4.1 is designed to make it easy to collate information from a variety of sources.

On reading the report it may be useful to:

- get your own copy of the recommendations section in full
- annotate the documentation provided by the SENCO
- make your own notes on relevant insights and information
- in the absence of an IEP or PP use Table 4.1 to record key information

Table 4.1 Core deficit – Specialist Report Digest

Pupil Name	Date of Report
Notes about baselines	Core deficits? Working memory, auditory processing? Processing speed, semantic knowledge? Surprises? Lowest scores? Has there been progress in a particular area over a specific period?
Subject specific concerns	Fine and gross motor/sensory problems might be a specific area of difficulty for Art, PE, Science, Food Tech Phonological processing affecting reading, writing, speaking and listening in English Concepts of time and number in Mathematics, science etc.

(Continued)

Table 4.1 (Continued)

Pupil Name	Date of Report
Cognitive strengths	High scores? Does the child have specific talents? What worked before and what do they enjoy? What are the child's aspirations? It often includes suggestions in terms of materials, tools and approaches to learning
Are there suggestions about the use of specific materials, books or technology?	Is there a specific strategy for giving instructions or managing behaviour? Are there specific triggers to avoid? (sensory or semantic)
Has this added to your understanding of the pupil and their family?	It may be that it is not appropriate to make notes after reading other than any action points to follow up.

In considering the admittedly time-consuming process of examining the details of a pupil's diagnostic paperwork above I was struck by the relevance and possible irony of a very useful element of reasoning the Drs Eide call 'gist'. They describe it as a strength in 'big-picture' or interconnected thinking that they have identified in young people and adults with dyslexia;

> the gist or overall message can't be determined by simply adding up' all the primary meanings of the words in the message, then computing the global meaning like a sum. Instead, the gist or overall meaning must be distilled carefully considering all the possible meanings of all the words and phrases, then determining the essence of the meaning as a whole.
>
> (Eide & Eide, 2011, p. 91)

How can I capture information about the underlying needs of a whole class?

Once you have distilled key messages about individuals it may be useful to reflect on the class group as a whole, especially in teaching groups with a high percentage of pupils with SpLD. It's possible that there are clearly identifiable subgroups emerging who have common underlying deficits or strengths. Collating this information in a simple form can assist in thinking through the possibilities for differentiation described in Chapter 7, informing considerations about grouping and resources etc.

Unfortunately, responding to diagnostic information is not as simple as adding up the numbers of pupils with a particular difficulty and addressing the most prevalent issue first. A specific difficulty represented by one pupil is as necessary to address as a difficulty shared by many. However, looking at the frequency and distribution of some common underlying deficits, like poor phonological awareness and slow processing time, can reveal an opportunity to enhance teaching for the entire group. This process of identifying the characteristics of the class group, including strengths, can inform routes into differentiation (discussed in Chapter 7) adding context to existing information about attainment. Use Table 4.2 to plot the frequency and distribution of core deficits in your class.

Table 4.2 Core deficit – class overview

Name	EP	SaLT	OT	Other	Working memory	Slow processing	Phonological Processing	Fine motor
Danny	x		x		D			
Chey								
Riley								
Ruben								
Adil								

When teaching a class where several children have identified difficulties it can be useful to look at the overview in order to adapt teaching.

There may be more than one kind of diagnostic assessment about a pupil.

What is a Speech and Language Assessment Report?

There is a significant distinction between assessment by an EP and a Speech and Language Therapist.

Assessment by a Speech and Language Therapist refers specifically to a child's speech, language and communication skills. While EPs tend to focus on tests of cognition, attainment, well-being and behaviour, Speech and Language Therapists can offer a forensic investigation of expressive and receptive language skills.

The category of Speech Language and Communication Need is consistently one of the largest subgroups identified in the SEND data; data produced in January 2017 recorded it as the second largest category in both primary and secondary phases. The need to build awareness and to maximise the impact of assessing children's speech, language and communication needs is underpinned by a number of factors. There is an established link between language and reading problems. The charity ICAN estimates that more than 90% of children identified as Speech Language and Communication Needs (SLCN) go on to have long-term problems[3] and possibly most disturbingly, consistent studies indicate a huge over-representation of people with SLCN in the prison population.[4]

Comprehensive assessments known as the Clinical Evaluation of Language Fundamentals Fourth Edition UK[5] (CELF4UK) are completed on a one-to-one basis and look in depth at key aspects of language development. A Speech and Language Assessment Report would follow a similar structure to any other specialist report: reason for referral and background, with test results followed by a summary and recommendations.

The CELF4UK produces a core language score. This standardised single score represents the pupil's language skills as a whole but, like the EP assessment and report, the CELF4UK provides numerous subtests and the report will provide scores and narrative feedback on each.

Areas of testing are likely to include:

- recalling and formulating sentences;
- word classes and word definitions;
- understanding spoken paragraphs;
- semantic relationships;
- sentence assembly;
- recalling sentences;
- working memory;
- verbal sequencing; and
- pragmatics (use of language).

The therapist may do a number of additional supplementary standardised tests focused on related aspects of functioning like auditory processing, receptive grammar and phonological processing.

What is an Occupational Therapy Assessment Report?

In layperson's terms an Occupational Therapist works in school to enable pupils to access the learning environment and to participate successfully in the day-to-day activities that make up school life, whether work, leisure or play.

Therapists work with children to develop everything from handwriting skills to using tools, materials and technology. Therapists may also have a role to play in developing a pupil's self-care for school: eating, dressing, toileting and general hygiene.

An Occupational Therapy referral may be made to assess any delay or difficulty in a child's fine and gross motor skills, visual perception or sensory integration affecting their participation, achievement and enjoyment of school.

Self-evaluation

What were the key messages from this chapter?

What do I need to review?

Which activities have I tried?

Which activities would I like to try?

Things I'd like to know more about:

Is this chapter relevant to a specific situation, pupil or class?

Notes

1 Detail of the WISC V can be found at the Pearson Clinical website: http://www.pearsonclinical.co.uk/ Psychology/ChildCognitionNeuropsychologyandLanguage/ChildGeneralAbilities/wisc-v/wechsler-intelligence-scale-for-children-fifth-uk-edtion-wisc-v-uk.aspx

2 British Dyslexia Association website: www.bdadyslexia.org.uk/educator/what-are-specific-learning-difficulties

3 See also the Talking Point, Impact of SLCN, ICAN website: www.talkingpoint.org.uk/slts/impact-slcn

4 Royal College of Speech and language Therapists, Speech language and Communication Needs in the Criminal Justice System – Dossier or Evidence January 2012.

5 Details from Pearson Clinical website: http://www.pearsonclinical.co.uk/Psychology/ChildCognition NeuropsychologyandLanguage/ChildLanguage/ClinicalEvaluationofLanguageFundamentals-FourthEditionUK(CELF-4UK)/ClinicalEvaluationofLanguageFundamentals-FourthEditionUK(CELF-4UK).aspx

Chapter 5

What is multi-sensory teaching?

This chapter offers the reader an explanation of the theory of multi-sensory teaching and its impact on the progress and attainment of pupils with Special Educational Needs Disability (SEND).

The reader is invited to take part in a series of activities with which to evaluate and audit the sensory aspects of their dominant teaching style and learning environment.

The chapter identifies the need for teachers to be mindful in the classroom and to consider the effect of the sensory diet on pupils learning in order to achieve a balance in terms of offering variety while avoiding over-stimulation and distraction.

What are the origins of a multi-sensory approach to teaching?

Children are brought up to believe that there are five basic human senses. Sight, hearing, taste, touch and smell have become ingrained in universal culture and permeate everything from children's books to TV, even teachers' scaffolding for creative writing. Possibly rooted in Aristotle's *De Anima*, the concept of five distinct categories of sensory input seems impervious to scientific discovery. A more current understanding of the senses separates sensory reception and perception, adds to and subdivides basic categories to include balance, thermo-reception and pain.

Historically, a multi-sensory approach refers to the philosophical concept of the five senses. A simple analogy for the use of a multi-sensory approach when teaching a pupil with learning difficulties characterises the brain as a filing cabinet. Each file drawer is labelled with the name of a different sense; sight, sound, touch, taste and smell. Multi-sensory teaching deliberately connects knowledge to an experience via one or more senses. Knowledge connected to more than one sense is therefore stored in more than one drawer; the more drawers in which knowledge is filed, the more likely the knowledge it is to be retrieved by the owner of the filing cabinet. Despite the oversimplification inherent in this model, recognition of the impact and mode of sensory input has earned a valid place in the discourse of Special Educational Needs (SEN) and proved useful and effective in enhancing teaching.

As the daughter of an East End vicar I often reflect on the multi-sensory environment of the church I attended throughout my childhood. It, like all religious institutions, was masterful in its use of multi-sensory pedagogy. Almost all religions to some extent involve ritualised used of oral language, music, movement, taste, smell and touch. Acts of worship invoke specific and general senses as each element signifies and reminds the worshipper of the next word, or a connotation and link to another action or idea. Religion has successfully harnessed the senses in a repetitive and deliberate effort to connect human experience to the ultimate abstract concept and done so with unparalleled success, ingraining belief in millions before there was a book in sight.

It would appear that the success of multi-sensory learning is less in the scientific analysis and more in the awareness of and response to impact.

At the beginning of the 20th century Samuel Orton and Anna Gillingham developed the Orton-Gillingham method to teach reading by explicitly linking letter sounds and shapes in a personalised and multi-sensory process, thus tailoring and optimising the learning experience by providing the learner with a variety of stimulus and the best possible chance of recall.

We commonly identify only five senses, but science has identified many more.

Historically, multi-sensory teaching exploits the links between the senses and memory.

Multi-sensory teaching is associated with the Orton-Gillingham system for teaching reading.

How is multi-sensory teaching used?

On diagnosing a pupil with SpLDs like dyslexia, EPs often recommend a programme of individualised support and tuition in a small group or one-to-one environment. These lessons are often tailor-made in order to address very specific gaps in areas like phonological knowledge, reading skills and handwriting, and often use a multi-sensory approach that acknowledges the pupil's perceptual strengths and weaknesses. It's generally accepted that a highly structured approach, combined with a variety of sensory stimulus, has proved to be an effective way to improve the literacy and general attainment of children who have struggled to make progress in a conventional whole-class setting.

How is multi-sensory teaching used by specialist teachers?

Specialist teacher training for teachers of pupils with SpLDs continues to promote a high level of specificity and personalisation. The post-graduate certificate course requires the teacher to design, develop and deliver a series of lessons in direct response to an ongoing diagnostic process that measures the impact of teaching in a gradual and cumulative process in which not only the pupil's knowledge but also their response and engagement in wide variety of tasks is carefully recorded and built into ongoing planning. Good specialist teaching is, and always has been, evidence-based and multi-sensory. Pupils are often encouraged to use a range of media including sand, wooden letters and putty to reproduce and reinforce the letter sounds and shapes they are attempting to master.

Isn't every classroom a multi-sensory classroom?

There is no doubt that the contemporary classroom is a multi-sensory environment. The rooms in which we teach are often multi-purpose spaces housing not only the tools of teaching but also the personal belongings and work product of the pupils and staff. In the last 20 years the only blank walls I see in schools are those in rooms scheduled for public examinations or demolition. The proliferation and availability of multimedia presentation means that children are exposed to an increasingly busy audio-visual environment for learning. The 21st-century learning space has burst into noisy Technicolor with a plethora of multimedia resources from audiobooks to YouTube.

Todays' classrooms are literally stuffed with possibilities. However, effective multi-sensory teaching, of the type described earlier, does not attract and engage all the senses indiscriminately. When using wooden letters to identify letter shapes or inviting the pupil to use a finger to draw a letter in sand, the teacher is deliberately introducing a sensory experience to focus and enhance a specific learning experience. Whether simply using colour, shaping numbers in putty or listening to a recording, the experience is designed to find a way to make a lasting memory for the pupil, to connect the knowledge to a sensory experience and thereby to fix it in the memory.

This type of teaching tends to take place in on a one-to-one basis or in small groups and is therefore often housed in a physical environment that differs in certain key respects from the mainstream classroom. Even in well-resourced, new-build schools, the rooms used to provide this kind of specialist, multi-sensory tuition are generally the smaller classrooms, sometimes little more than cupboards and cubicles. They tend to be spaces where it is easier to be selective about sensory input and to include stimuli by choice rather than by accident. This contrasts with the colour, light, sound, movement and frenetic activity that is the modern mainstream classroom.

To be able to select and offer a sensory experience to support learning in the mainstream classroom, teachers need to be able to reduce and to deselect sensory stimulus as much as to select and include it.

In specialist teaching, aspects of the sensory experience are controlled and directed by the teacher.

It can be difficult to control and direct multi-sensory teaching in mainstream classrooms.

How can I regulate the classroom environment?

It may be that to optimise learning opportunities for pupils with learning difficulties we need to think more about how the environment affects our pupils and to consider the ways we can modify it to enhance the learning experience rather than adding to its sensory variety.

Schools have a great deal of experience in this. In public examinations we apply strict regulations to the classroom. We have an obligation to the Joint Council for Qualifications to follow their strict guidance in controlling the physical environment. It's necessary to eliminate talking, reduce and control noise, reduce visual stimulus, introduce space, eliminate food, control drink, and include specific facilities like clocks and signage. This is done to optimise the likelihood of a genuinely independent response and to optimise performance and focus by reducing distractions.

A classroom under 'exam conditions' serves to illustrate three things: the power of the learning environment to influence pupil behaviour; the classroom as a blank canvas, stripped back to basics; the contrast that exists between a typical environment for learning and a typical environment for recall. It may be that finding opportunities for 'multi-sensory' teaching requires an active approach towards regulating the sensory environment of the classroom. Looking at default settings and variables is a place to start.

The audit in Table 5.1 invites you to think about the sensory environment in your current teaching room or rooms. It identifies the components of the current set-up and the rationale, and identifies the variables in order to consider how often this environment is deliberately varied and the impact this has on learning.

Use Table 5.1 to think about the rooms in which you teach.

If you work in a team or with a TA it is worth asking them to complete the table independently. It may also be possible to collect this information from the pupils to test your assumptions and build self-awareness in terms of learning behaviour.

Table 5.1 Sensory audit of the classroom/teaching space

Environment	Does this vary depending on the activity?	How often does it vary?	Can this be improved?	Action
Lights: source and level	Yes	There are areas of the classroom and times of the day when there is low-level light, or the lights are dimmed and switched off.	This has a calming effect on James.	
Temperature	No	Windows can be opened.		
Seating	Yes	Rarely		
Space between furniture				
Height and angle of tables				
Use of headphones				
Orientation of room				
Air circulation				
Time spent in one attitude				
Seating plan				
View of the boards				
Access to basic materials				

How do I balance the need for visual or multi-sensory cues against possible distractions?

The paradox inherent in teaching pupils with SpLDs is that a multi-sensory approach is necessary for success but too much stimulation can be a bad thing.

It is necessary to achieve a balance between opportunities for thought, processing and recall so that they do not become added opportunities for significant distraction. Complete with slogans and posters, key words and progression charts, school walls can look more like advertisements for learning than spaces for thought, experimentation and concentration.

Having access to visual cues is not the same as being surrounded by them. To achieve a balance in regulating the multi-sensory approach it may be necessary to supplement learning selectively and sequentially rather than offering a variety of cues simultaneously.

The Resources section of Chapter 7 provides a tool to review the visual cues available in the classroom called the 'visual cues audit'. This has become a regular feature of differentiation training and an activity that teachers can do immediately in their own classrooms. Spending some time looking at the walls, desks and caddies of laminated material provides teachers benefit because they have an opportunity to reflect on the use, the purpose and success of the tools at hand in delivering desired outcomes.

 Awareness of the sensory stimuli available can help teachers to regulate the classroom environment and support pupils with learning difficulties.

What is a sensory diet?

Pupils who need sensory diets add another dimension to considerations to be made about the classroom environment and its routines. Building on the principle that accommodations don't necessarily need to be differences, it's possible that a change for everyone can help to include a child without making them feel different. It's likely that while a child requires specific types of additional sensory input to help them cope with concentration in the mainstream classroom they or others may also require a degree of protection against over stimulation or specific triggers.

It's helpful to have a sensory toolbox ready to try, including:

- **a variety of manipulatives** like koosh balls and tangles; these can sooth and focus pupils who otherwise may seek sensory feedback by chewing sleeves or shredding books and paper or looking for spare equipment to manipulate;
- **Wobble cushions** and **resistance bands** for chairs to help pupils who find it difficult to maintain core stability when seated and tend to move around on their chair or in the room;
- **grips** for pens and pencils to make writing and drawing more comfortable;
- **headphones,** which can be used to focus on recordings or excluding sound; and
- **latex desk surfaces** to grip paper and make writing and drawing more comfortable.

These individual measures can have significant and relatively instant impact and send a message that the classroom is an adaptable and welcoming place. If the teacher is able to participate and incorporate the use of such a tool this can help to normalise what might otherwise stand out as an adaptation.

How do I make compliance easy?

Sensory issues can be most obvious when addressing the class as a whole. The way we signal certain routines and how we carry them out can make compliance easy or difficult. Its in the interest of all children to build in measures that make compliance with rules easy. Creating routines in which all can participate is often an easier choice than making an exception. The benefit of a specific adaptation can be quickly negated for a child if their peers perceive adjustments to be unfair.

Ultimately school should support the development of independence for the child with learning difficulties so while additional resources and one-to-one support may be available, a five-minute audit of classroom routines could ascertain if adjustments can in fact be made to existing routines to find a solution that works for all the pupils. Routines might include those listed in Table 5.2.

Table 5.2 Sensory audit of the classroom routines

Routine	Issue	Adaption for All
Lesson changes/bells	Alarm, loud noises	Leave lesson early, seating, earphone, change bell sound
Greeting	Disruption when pupils stand to greet	Seated greeting
Seating		
Lining up for breaks		
Dressing for PE		
Packing kit		
Homework bag		
Assembly		
Eating lunch		
Clearing up		

What can I do to support pupils with specific sensory needs?

Pupils with autistic spectrum conditions may well have closely documented sensory triggers. Children can have extreme sensitivity to triggers as diverse as cardboard or *Doctor Who*. Exposure to such triggers can send them fleeing from the classroom in serious distress. Doing your homework, as the previous chapter suggests, is helpful in avoiding these kinds of incidents; however, there is still the need to be aware that this response may arise in relation to other stimuli as yet unknown. Only close attention to the diagnostic data, along with trial and error based on good feedback from support staff and from home, can develop this essential provision as the child moves through the curriculum.

It's helpful to have a sensory toolbox available.

Classroom routines are part of the pupil's sensory experience and as such require consideration.

Specialist support is available when supporting pupils.

What can I do to support pupils with Visual and Hearing Impairment?

It's more common for pupils with sensory impairment to be supported by a specialist Visual Impairment (VI) or Hearing Impairment (HI) specialist who can offer advice on technology including radio-mics, laptops and supplementary materials. Good communication with home and the specialist can support excellent practice. There is no replacement for awareness of the diagnostic materials and seeking regular feedback from pupils themselves in order to ensure that they are comfortable with provision and can access all aspects of the curricular and extra-curricular offer.

Self-evaluation

What were the key messages from this chapter?

What do I need to review?

Which activities have I tried?

Which activities would I like to try?

Things I'd like to know more about:

Is this chapter relevant to a specific situation, pupil or class?

Chapter 6

Who are DR GOPTA and MR CHUFFI?

This chapter takes its name from a couple of light-hearted mnemonics referring to seven widely used routes into differentiation and linking them to seven frequently identified features of outstanding teaching.

The chapter sets out the features and impact of the most effective teaching practices. It makes the case that access to such teaching for all pupils, particularly those with learning difficulties, is dependent on effective differentiation. The premise is that without a clear focus for differentiation in the classroom, 'meeting need' can translate in to keeping pupils with learning difficulties on task or occupied.

The chapter then takes each of the seven routes into differentiation in turn and invites the reader to reflect on their current knowledge and practice in each respect. The text is punctuated by checklists, audits and training activities designed to help the reader find new opportunities to link the differentiation agenda spelled out by DR GOPTA to the agenda for effective teaching and learning spelled out by MR CHUFFI.

What are the features of effective teaching according to the DFE Teaching Standards 2011?

Logic dictates that a model of good practice for teachers is implicit in the 2011 National Standards for teachers published by the DFE, prefaced by this statement:

> Teachers make the education of their pupils their first concern, and are accountable for achieving the highest possible standards in work and conduct. Teachers act with honesty and integrity; have strong subject knowledge, keep their knowledge and skills as teachers up-to-date and are self-critical; forge positive professional relationships; and work with parents in the best interests of their pupils.
>
> (DFE, 2011)

The Standards subdivide into two sections: Standards for Teaching and Standards for Personal and Professional Conduct.

The 35 teaching standards are divided into eight sections: setting high expectations; promoting good progress and outcomes; good subject and curricular knowledge; planning and teaching well-structured lessons; responding to the strengths and needs of all students; accurate and useful assessment; managing behaviour to ensure a safe environment; and the responsibility to take part in the wider life of the school.

Section 5 of the standards is concerned with the specific responsibility to address the 'strengths and needs' (DFE, 2011) of all students. Expectations on teachers again are high and include the ability to:

- differentiate appropriately;
- use effective approaches to teaching;
- know how to overcome a range of factors that inhibit learning;
- be aware of the physical, social and intellectual aspects of child development;
- recognise and adapt teaching to support pupils' education at different stages of development; and
- have a clear understanding of the needs of all pupils (Special Educational Needs Disability [SEND], Gifted and Talented and English as an Additional Language) and be able to use and evaluate distinctive teaching approaches to engage and support them.

What are the features of effective teaching according to the Inspectorate?

The features of 'Outstanding' teaching identified by Ofsted comprise elements of behavioural, constructivist and ecological theory. Inspection frameworks for observing lessons have historically presented the features of outstanding lessons according to four categories, noting key features of the environment and the features of the learning taking place in conjunction with the activities and habits of teacher and pupils. The recently reviewed *Handbook for Inspection* describes 'Outstanding' teaching, learning and assessment in detail (Ofsted, 2017b, p. P51). There appears to be a renewed emphasis on depth, both in terms of teacher knowledge, aspirations and feedback, and in terms of the resilience, intellectual curiosity, and demands placed on all pupils to become better and more ambitious independent learners.

The teaching standards set high expectations for teachers to respond to the needs of all students.

Features of 'Outstanding' teaching should be available to all pupils via differentiated teaching.

How can effective teaching be measured?

It is worth noting that while models of effective teaching continue to evolve and the official terminology changes (High Quality Teaching, Quality First Teaching), research into measures of teacher effectiveness, while consistently identifying key practices, is frank about its shortcomings. While pupil outcomes remain a school's key concern, there are inherent difficulties in measuring teacher effectiveness defined purely in those terms. A recent study 'Effective Teaching', produced by the Education Development Trust with the University of Hong Kong and Oxford University, concluded 'that defining teacher effectiveness is not a simple matter' (Ko, et al., 2014, p. 52). The report identified that the most commonly used strategies of lesson observation, analysis of pupil outcomes, pupil voice and inspection could be enhanced by greater nuance and the recognition of several key variables.

Are there specific models of effective teaching for pupils with SpLD and SEND?

A Department for Education and Skills (DFES) publication from 2004 specifically investigated effective SEN teaching with the aim to 'map out and assess the effectiveness of the different approaches and strategies used to teach pupils with the full range of SEN' (DFES, 2004, p. 7). The report reviewed research and set out to identify promising teaching strategies for each category of SEN, according to the category of SEND, the dominant theoretical perspectives and the phase of teaching.

The theoretical perspectives encompassed constructivist, behavioural and ecological theories of learning.

The findings of this report support and subsequent educational policy reflect the need for teachers to combine aspects of educational theory rather than to adopt a single model: 'there is a growing understanding of the need to move away from the belief that one model of learning informs and justifies one model of teaching' (DFES, 2004, p. 19). If we accept that a separate and specific pedagogy for meeting the needs of pupils with SEND is a redundant question, we are left to consider the following questions: To what extent are the conditions and practices in place for a meaningful inclusive model? Also, to what extent do pupils with SEN experience the best teaching and learning practice school has to offer?

The conditions for successful inclusion, set out by Florian in the 1990s, remain at the heart of the current Code of Practice:

- pupil voice;
- positive attitude about ability;
- teacher knowledge about learning difficulties;
- skill in specific teaching methods; and
- parent/teacher support.

(Florian, et al., 1998)

However, after 20 years of reform designed to legislate for and facilitate an inclusive model of education, teachers still struggle to find their own, unique solutions to meeting the needs of pupils with SEN in the context of developing outstanding classroom practice.

This chapter is designed to offer teachers structured support in making explicit links between their knowledge and understanding of SEND, the features of teaching practice consistently identified as the most effective, and a structure for differentiation that affords pupils with specific learning disabilities (SpLD) and SEND genuine access to an inclusive classroom experience.

With a view to making manageable sense of the standards and expectations outlined earlier in this chapter, and to simplify the process of planning, I have modified and added to the core agenda of effective teaching practices identified in the DISS report. See DISS project briefing note 4 on interactions between teaching assistants and pupils. I have called it the MR CHUFFI agenda. MR CHUFFI spells out a teaching and learning agenda derived from a mixed pedagogical approach, designed to promote the intellectual depth, challenge, curiosity, self-awareness and resilience so apparent in models of excellent teaching practice. It looks to ensure that pupils with SpLD and SEND do not get trapped at the lower levels of Bloom's Taxonomy but are encouraged to attempt evaluative, creative and analytical tasks. Each letter of MR CHUFFI represents a feature of practice that has multiple resonance and relevance to teaching and learning:

1   Making Links
2   Risk taking
3   Cognitive engagement
4   Higher-level thinking
5   Checking Understanding
6   Frequent Feedback
7   Fostering Independence

To be fully included and to succeed at school, pupils with SEND require the same access to these features of effective teaching and learning as their neurotypical classmates. If their participation in a mainstream classroom is to lead to achievement, sustained motivation and opportunity, the inclusion agenda cannot stop at the classroom door: it must extend directly into the teaching and learning experience.

Teaching should be multi-modal and inclusive of children with SEND.

Conditions for inclusion identified in the 1990s are still valid today.

MR CHUFFI sets an aspirational agenda for teaching pupils with learning difficulties, derived from research, guidance and experience.

Pupils with learning difficulties require access to the most effective features of teaching and learning.

What should effective differentiation do?

According to the teaching standards and the Inspectorate, differentiation enables pupils to be taught effectively by using a range of strategies and approaches chosen and adapted to meet the full range of learners' needs. The expectation is that all pupils, including those with SpLDs and SEN, will then enjoy the same features of outstanding teaching and learning as their non-SEND classmates.

The process works on two levels. Put in its simplest terms, to differentiate is:

•   to acknowledge and to try to understand the differences between one pupil and another; and
•   to take the appropriate action to ensure that difference does not necessarily become disadvantage.

Clearly, a learning difficulty often creates a divide between the pupil and the experience of academic success. Effective differentiation must be a bridge crossing that divide. It should encourage pupils to use and to enhance their abilities while recognizing, acknowledging and developing strategies to mitigate them.

In our haste to address identified difficulties it's easy to overlook the fact that children with learning difficulties are also children with learning abilities. One does not preclude the other. When learning difficulties are specific, this pattern of contrasting strengths and weaknesses is an inherent characteristic. The teacher's recognition of a pupil's ability, interest, curiosity and motivation is pivotal in building the resilience needed to progress. Differentiation should not be designed to occupy, pacify or placate pupils but to engage them in learning and to motivate them to achieve. Considering the significant and substantial contribution of people with SpLDs and SEND to our society it is disappointing that greater emphasis is not placed on identifying and optimising their obvious strengths.

In the book *The Dyslexic Advantage* (Eide & Eide, 2011) Drs Ross and Fernette Eide outline for compensatory and complimentary cognitive strengths they have observed in children and adults diagnosed with dyslexia. They argue that these strengths lie in material, interconnected, narrative and dynamic reasoning (MIND) and present case studies and research to support their theory. Their approach and research adds a new and positive dimension to considerations for differentiated teaching, highlighting the need to ensure academic aspirations for pupils with SpLD and SEND remain high.

Children with learning difficulties are also children with learning abilities.

Pupils with SpLDs require an approach to differentiation that takes account of their cognitive strengths.

Differentiation should engage pupils in learning and lead to achievement.

How can I lead on differentiation to ensure a high-quality teaching and learning experience for pupils with SpLD and SEN?

DR GOPTA is an acronym indicating seven well-known routes into differentiation:

1 Dialogue
2 Resources
3 Grouping
4 Outcome
5 Pace
6 Task
7 Assessment

The model for differentiation is one I have come across frequently in practice and training, and a modification of the one explained by Jayne Bartlett in her book, *Outstanding Differentiation for Learning in the Classroom* (Bartlett, 2016).

In this framework, differentiation and meeting the need of pupils with SEN is led by teachers, and it promotes an essential role of the classroom teacher in leading learning for all children. Research material produced over the last decade concerning the deployment of TAs has shown that the academic progress of pupils with learning difficulties has often been inhibited rather than enhanced by their offer of generalised support. Notwithstanding this evidence, the role of the TA as differentiator-in-chief is perpetuated in too many settings. For TAs to add value to teaching and contribute to pupil progress and attainment it's necessary for them to receive specific training, and to possess a good level of understanding of both learning difficulties and the strategies and features of teaching that have proved most effective. The role of TAs in supporting this agenda is covered in the next chapter.

Almost without exception, the teachers, support staff and school leaders I meet agree on the need for new and more effective solutions to teaching pupils with learning difficulties. They face an ever-increasing diversity of need within the context of limited and shrinking resources. With that in mind, the brand of differentiation I propose in this book is one designed to enhance the performance of staff within existing resources – one that advocates good habits for smarter working. This is differentiation as a refinement of teaching rather than a proliferation of activity and cost.

It's easy to get lost in the hunt for additional resources and programmes that might provide a quick fix – a short-term gain, a busy child, some quiet, a focus, a finished piece of work. While 'filler' activities, often those with low cognitive challenge, can be used to manage a classroom, they are unlikely to build knowledge and understanding or indeed specific skills without thoughtful pre-arrangement, planning and design.

Returning to the original question of what differentiation should do, the cover-all answer is that 'gaps' would close and that pupils with learning difficulties would progress and attain in line with their peers. However, it's likely that progression for children with learning difficulties may be a slow and uneven path. Determining appropriate expectations and accurate predictions for pupils with learning difficulties requires a degree of thoughtful consideration, time and expert support. To make the MR CHUFFI agenda available for pupils with learning difficulties, goals for learning must be agreed which look not only to attainment but that recognise the mode and level of the pupil's engagement in independent learning.

 Differentiation is most effective when led by teachers.

Differentiation can be a refinement of existing practice.

Good habits for differentiation begin with reflection and self-evaluation.

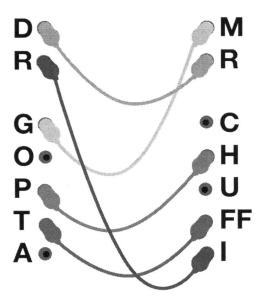

Illustration 6.1 Effective differentiation meets effective teaching

Source: James Gray

How can DR GOPTA help pupils to access the MR CHUFFI agenda?

MR CHUFFI and DR GOPTA are two simple and deliberately silly mnemonics that offer a memorable framework for teachers, and thereby keep in mind the goals, the means and the opportunities that exist in every classroom for effective and consistent differentiation.

To ensure that pupils with SEND enjoy the opportunities afforded by the most effective teaching, represented by the MR CHUFFI agenda, we need the help of our friend DR GOPTA, each letter of the mnemonic referring to an opportunity to assist the struggling learner. Illustration 6.1 shows the interconnectivity of the two agendas.

Thinking about dialogue

I use the word 'dialogue' to refer to and to emphasise the nature of teaching as a conversation involving two or more people. This path into differentiation could just as well be called communication, oracy or just plain talk. Its focus is on how we can make deliberate choices about the way we use talk in our classrooms from early years to sixth form – how we instruct, explain and question – but as importantly how we listen and how we encourage and develop the skills of our pupils to participate in and benefit from this ongoing dialogue.

You could be forgiven for thinking that the only pupils requiring special consideration and support in this respect would be those identified as having specific speech, language and communication needs (SLCN). However, unfortunately that's not the case.

It's necessary to consider what we have already learned about the matrix of interconnected needs that often forms an SpLD diagnosis and the likely impact of its common features: difficulties with processing time, phonological processing, auditory memory and working memory. Chapter 4 drew attention to the fact that pupils with a wide variety of SpLDs struggle with all of these.

Talk and working memory

Ross and Tracy Alloway have done much to explore the impact of working memory on learning and life chances. In their book *The Working Memory Advantage* they describe its function as the brain's 'conductor', working to retain, prioritise and process information to 'do something with the information at hand rather than just remember it briefly' (Alloway & Alloway, 2013, p. 8). One aspect of working memory is a 'phonological loop' which deals with holding and storing spoken and written material. Children with poor working memory affecting this 'loop' may find it more difficult than most to recall specific information and instructions they need while focused on a new problem or a piece of work. If their phonological processing skills are also weak, it's likely to affect the quality of information received – and the two problems come together in their ability to manage the demands of the classroom.

Oracy and literacy

Dyslexia is most commonly associated with difficulties in reading, writing and spelling. Sometimes pupils are initially identified by an apparent discrepancy between a child's ability to articulate their thoughts in speech and their apparent inability to 'get those ideas on paper' or indeed to read about them independently.

The complex relationship between literacy and language problems is not often a focus of SEN training in schools. It's easy to see why teachers and parents expect aptitude in oracy and literacy to be consistent, however, it's vital for educators to acknowledge this inconsistency. While speaking, listening and writing are all aspects of language, the perceptual, production, processing and memory skills involved in their development are not one and the same; they can be specifically, uniquely uneven or impaired. A pupil with an above average spelling score is not immune to an underlying language problem with any number of aspects from semantics or receptive grammar and a pupil with huge reading and writing difficulties may have the ability to reason well verbally and speak using a wide range of vocabulary. The danger is in making assumptions about ability or difficulty and not testing those assumptions.

Talk and undiagnosed problems

I was well into my second job in special needs teaching before I even met a Speech and Language Therapist. I was a SENCO before I began to understand the profoundly negative impact that expressive and receptive language difficulties can have on the development of speaking, listening, reading and writing in the classroom.

While awareness and training in this respect have improved since the early days of my career, there is some urgency that schools develop the skills to recognise the impact of undiagnosed language and communication difficulties. Statistics published by the Communication Trust[1] show 60% of people in the criminal justice system have language and communication needs as opposed to 5% of the general population. Without better understanding and more effective support at school there is little to stop the growth of this massive overrepresentation. This makes it imperative for teachers of all subjects and phases to acknowledge the importance of language development and to consider the possibility of an underlying problem, notwithstanding a pupil's tendency to chat superficially, be very quiet and compliant, to use aggression to deflect attention or to avoid talking by being disruptive.

Repetition and re-enforcement

The 21st-century mainstream classroom is an overwhelmingly auditory environment in which talk is often the 'go to' method for repetition and reinforcement offered to the struggling learner. However, if the struggle to learn has at its root a specific difficulty in language processing, while verbatim repetition from a TA or the class teacher may help the pupil to cope at the time without screening and intervention it is unlikely to resolve this problem for the pupil.

Classroom Talk Audit

The Classroom Talk Audit shown in Table 6.1 can be used to find out how much you know about the way you use talk and how much classroom talk works to support the MR CHUFFI agenda. It's a tool for reflection and could be used self-reflectively after teaching, after listening back to a recorded lesson or completed by a teaching colleague, TA, LSA, or pupil. It's also possible to do a prediction first and then compare it to feedback after the event. It may be that you might want to compare the way you teach across disciplines or with different groups to see how much variation there is.

The feedback should give you some useful insights into your existing use of talk and an indication of the opportunities to differentiate your current practice for the benefit of those in your children in your class with learning difficulties.

Table 6.1 Classroom Talk Audit

	Often = O; Sometimes = S; Never = N	O/S/N
	I use ...	**Rating**
Introduce, repeat and re-enforce important spoken vocabulary	Be selective and explicit when introducing new words.	
	Break down words into syllables verbal and visual (presentation).	
	Explain where the word comes from.	
	Explore and explain how it is linked to this and other subjects.	
	Can it be visually represented – pictogram?	
	Is prefix and suffix helpful to note?	
	Use word often and consistently – both say and show.	
	Offer all of the above more than once using same language to avoid confusion.	
	Reward correct use of word rather than correct spelling out of context.	
Encourage active listening	Show attention	
	Show empathy	
	Manage non-verbal communication	
	Paraphrase	

(Continued)

Table 6.1 (Continued)

	Often = O; Sometimes = S; Never = N	A/S/N
	I use ...	Rating
	Summarise	
	Play barrier games	
	Play word or phrase bingo	
Questioning	Show attention	
	Show empathy and acceptance	
	Manage non-verbal communication	
	Paraphrase	
	Summarise	
	Play barrier games	
	Reward active listening	
Encourage Speaking	Provide opportunities for pupils to talk, comment, reflect and question.	
	Don't allow seating plan and classroom geography to create random constraints.	
	Use 'mantle of the expert'.	

	Often = O; Sometimes = S; Never = N	A/S/N
	I use ...	Rating
Vary listening focus/ voice	Pupil voice	
	TA	
	Books on tape	
	Radio and podcasts	
	Community voices	
Address grammar in speech by offering	Corrections	
	Explanations	
	Rewards	
Vary volume, tone and register	Model appropriate tone and register	
	Manage volume	
	Identify inside outside, individual and group voices	

Following the Classroom Talk Audit – look at the areas you've rated as Sometimes or Never. Consider what new opportunities there might be to enable a pupil with learning difficulties to Make Links, Risk Take, Cognitively Engage, Engage Higher Level Thinking, Check Understanding, Feedback or Foster Independence.

How can I introduce and build vocabulary?

Vocabulary is a cornerstone of attainment at school. Without the requisite semantic knowledge, it's impossible to unlock the curriculum independently. While there are technological devices that can read to you, spell for you and record audio-visual documents of your experience, the business of translating language into meaning requires an individual to develop a secure and ever-widening vocabulary. How vocabulary is introduced, learned and embedded is a relevant question for all teachers in all phases.

The checklist in Table 6.2 encourages a belt-and-braces approach; assuming that vocabulary is *not* in place without explicit attention, repetition and reference to context provides the best possible support to those who are often least able to express the specifics of their struggle.

Table 6.2 Vocabulary planning

Opportunities	Behaviour	Opportunity
Vocabulary	Be selective and explicit when introducing new words.	
	Break down words into syllables verbal and visual presentation.	
	Explain where the word comes from.	
	Explore and explain how it is linked to this and other subjects.	
	Can it be visually represented – pictogram?	
	Are common prefixes and suffixes helpful to explore?	
	Use the word often and consistently – both say and show.	
	Offer all of the above repeatedly – come back to new words.	
	Reward pupil's use of the word in correct context.	

How can I encourage active listening?

Models of effective listening tend to include the following:

Attention. Attention[2] is something that teachers expect, even demand, but do we know it when we see it? It may be that our pupils show their attention differently. Most classroom teachers expect children to show attention by refraining from talk themselves, by making eye contact, facing towards the speaker and restricting movement or being still. However, there may well be pupils who struggle so much with maintaining the conditions required to show attention that they have no energy left for actual listening. Look around your average staff meeting, and you will see any number of adults shifting in their seats, whispering, doodling, folding, chewing and shredding – as adults we tend to find discrete ways to accommodate our sensory needs. It's healthy to want to move around, to leave a screen because you are full of movement. The use of doodling, manipulatives, chew toys, wobble cushions and foot fidget devises can all be extremely useful in soothing and supporting the attention of children with attention and sensory needs, but their use has to be informed, agreed and monitored.

Empathy. I think of empathy as more an underlying motivation than as a specific skill to be practiced. Having some care for how it feels to be in the pupil's position, without taking that position, is a good basis on which to develop good practice in regards the classroom conversation. The most successful teachers remember how it feels to be a learner and the vulnerability that can go with that, how it feels to ask questions and to be questioned, to share ideas and to be judged in the public forum that is any classroom.

Acceptance. I wrote a piece for a magazine a couple of years ago about what we say to pupils when they are wrong. Even the word 'wrong' feels value-laden and judgemental. There has been much progress in classrooms and much debate about how to celebrate first attempt at learning. Some classrooms now have displays that celebrate the learning journey and contextualise staff and pupil mistakes as opportunities. This kind of accepting approach can be more difficult to balance in the everyday exchange of ideas and information that takes place in verbal communication. When talking to a group the need to be clear has to be balanced with an attempt to be accepting. A positive approach can be a helpful tool, especially in attempting to defuse situations of opposition or conflict. Instead of 'you' statements characterising the other person's mistake or error it can be helpful to try something more positive: 'I understand that's how you feel' and 'I accept that you have formed that opinion' can be neutralising ways in.

Non-verbal behaviour. This is everything we are doing while we are not talking. It's estimated that more than half of communication is non-verbal. Making choices about how we position ourselves physically, the time we give to speaking and to listening, how we make eye contact and use facial expression has a direct impact on dialogue. These things can be either a welcome encouragement to take the risk and talk or a discouragement from doing so or, worse still, an exclusion from the exchange. Pupils who struggle to read non-verbal behaviour, because of their difficulties, may well benefit from direct instruction in building a vocabulary for gesture and hand signals (Makaton[3]) to accompany common instructions.

Paraphrasing. This feature has a particular usefulness in coaching conversations but is also an essential and helpful tool in the classroom, particularly for the struggling pupil. A paraphrase is an attempt to reflect something accurately that has been said, without adding advice or opinion. It's a tool that is often used to ensure the clarity and shared understanding of what has been said. Practicing paraphrasing can be a particularly useful exercise but is often more difficult than it would appear. In general conversation, we rarely listen and respond to a speaker without adding something of our own experience or opinion. A paraphrase requires us actively to do neither but to simply reflect back to the speaker what has just been said. A script for this can be useful at first. It can be introduced with, 'if I understand you correctly', 'you seem to be saying', 'am I right in thinking' before going on to repeat back to the speaker what they have just said. In doing this you are carefully checking understanding while showing that you have listened carefully to the speaker. It seems so simple but can be a surprisingly powerful tool in communicating empathy while underpinning clarity and offering an opportunity for repetition. These are all good for a pupil who struggles with language skills – expressive or receptive – or who has difficulty with short-term auditory memory.

Summarising. This is distinct from paraphrasing in that it brings together in brief a complete summary of the material that has been covered in a conversation or an exchange. It can be used in coaching to set out the choices in terms of the focus for a session or perhaps in deciding on priorities. Summarising is a skill that we often work on with pupils to develop but it can have real usefulness in supporting pupils who struggle with auditory memory. To recall and recap the content of a class discussion or question-and-answer session, setting out not only the end point but revisiting the stages on that journey provides a useful opportunity to think through and revisit the experience and the sequence of events. Eide and Eide talk at length in their book *The Dyslexic Advantage* about how classroom learning can be hampered by over-reliance on breaking things down into small chunks and the danger of losing reference to the 'bigger picture' (Eide & Eide, 2011, p. 51). The connections between the stages of a learning journey are important in securing recall. By using summary in this way to recap and rehearse a class discussion the teachers can help to support working memory and referring to the bigger picture context.

Advice. In a conversation we often look to advise or share our opinions rather than to give instructions. In the classroom it's important to be clear which of the two we are offering. Remembering that this section is about good listening skills, and that the advice offered in class is distinct from the instructions that pupils receive. Advice should be personalised, nuanced and have the quality of guidance. It might be worth thinking how differently a piece of advice might be phrased so that a pupil can consider it but retain some judgement and choice over what to do next. 'What would you think about including this idea? Have you thought about using colour here?' Advice makes an offer, it doesn't take control.

Barrier games. Barrier games focus the players completely on effective expressive and receptive language. It is often a subject of great hilarity for teachers when practising these games in training to realise how difficult it is to cope with auditory only input.

Training activity

1   Sit facing away from your partner, back to back works best.
2   Player 1 uses four colours to draw four shapes on to a piece of paper. The shapes can be separate or overlap.
3   Player 1 offers verbal instructions to Player 2 so that s/he may replicate the drawing.
4   Player 2 follows Player 1's instructions in the attempt to replicate the drawing, but should not ask questions.
5   Compare drawings and notes on formulating instruction.

Clearly the material described by Player 1 does not have to be shapes. You can create a barrier game for any subject or phase dependent on your choice of source material – allowing you to promote, practise and consolidate specific skills and specific words.

Reward Active listening. Rewarding the processes of learning rather than outcomes alone emphasises key skills necessary for independent learning.

How can I optimise the use of questions?

While it's likely that there will be specific routines in place ensuring that all pupils participate in classroom conversations, when you use systems that randomise and circulate the opportunity to speak – picking out named lolly sticks from a jar, passing or throwing or catching a ball – it's less likely that there is a system in place to help you to monitor, vary and develop your style of questioning and to judge the impact of that variety on the distribution and quality of pupils' verbal responses.

Table 6.3 Active listening

Opportunities	Behaviour	Opportunity
Encourage active listening	Show attention	
	Show empathy and acceptance	
	Manage non-verbal communication	
	Paraphrase	
	Summarise	
	Play barrier games	
	Reward active listening	

Questioning is a key aspect of the classroom conversation. There are many different types of questions, designed to elicit a variety of response. Both open and closed questions can be used to promote the MR CHUFFI agenda for children with learning difficulties. Inclusion and participation in the daily Q and A of classroom life has to be a cornerstone of inclusion.

It's essential to recognise the difference between questions that open up a dialogue and questions that close or complete the conversation. In every classroom there is space for both. The skill lies in being aware of the nature and variety of your questioning techniques and their impact on learning.

Open questions can often elicit a descriptive and sustained response; open questions require the subject to think, to describe and to share their understanding, inviting a fuller, more linguistically complex response. An open question can often be phrased simply by using what, why, how or invitations like 'tell me about', 'describe' and so on.

Closed questions often lead to one-word answers: 'yes', 'no' or 'don't know' or the provision of a fact.

Training activity

The aim of this activity is to practice and develop a repertoire of open questions.

1 Working in pairs, Player 1 can choose any subject to speak on, their favourite band, the journey to work, Brexit (maybe not) – Player 2 must sustain the conversation, intervening only with open questions. Player 2 must make every effort to avoid a closed question and to refrain from statements sharing experiences, knowledge and opinions.
2 Feedback to each other on the process. Swap and repeat.

How can I create thinking time?

Dialogue doesn't have to be instant. A verbal question once posed need not be answered immediately; the first hands don't necessarily produce the best answers. However, it's interesting to note that in the vast majority of learning walks I've undertaken the speed of pupil response is equated with ability, enthusiasm and successful class discussion. Making space for a 'slow burn', in terms of verbal response, is a simple way to include children with learning difficulties in higher order thinking and encourage well-constructed expressive language. This can be structured in any number of ways including peer deliberation to come up with an agreed response, allowing a practice response to be worked through with a TA, returning to a single question throughout the lesson and offering a scaffold or starters for phrasing.

Rewards

A rewards system that highlights the value of interesting and effective questions, good listening and turn taking is as helpful in modelling purposeful and effective classroom conversations.

Visual cues

To support slow burners, scaffold speech and offer starters. It is likely that supplementary resources are going to be useful. Visual or auditory cues can of course take the burden away from working memory and allow a child to come back to the parked information. Dry-wipe boards, sticky notes or recordings of important questions can all be useful in keeping thinking on track and making it possible to take part in the discussion.

Table 6.4 Asking questions

Opportunities	Behaviour	Opportunity
Questions	Explain open and closed questions.	
	Use a mixture of open and closed questions.	
	Vary thinking time for verbal responses (slow burners).	
	Reward useful pupil questions.	
	Provide visual cues for high-frequency questions.	

How can I encourage speaking?

Making space for children to speak and to be heard has never been more important, particularly in the light of feedback from teachers in primary schools and early years settings who express growing concern about the impact of the smartphone and tablet on the language and educational development of young children and family life in general. Clearly advances in communication technology offer pupils with severe speech language and communication and/or physical needs very obvious and exciting opportunities, in the form of voice- and eye-activated technologies. However, concern surrounds the potential disadvantages of excessive use of the more widely available technologies and has prompted a very public discourse amongst professionals about how to advise schools and parents and to best manage the phenomenon.[4] While the jury continues to be out it would seem sensible to be vigilant and to ensure that school-age children with learning difficulties have the optimum opportunity to participate in and to benefit from the rich social environment of the classroom and are offered the broadest opportunity to develop social communication skills, and are regularly and actively encouraged to speak.

Table 6.5 Encouraging speaking

Opportunities	Behaviour	Opportunity
Encourage speaking	Provide opportunities for pupils to talk, comment, reflect and question.	
	Don't allow seating plan and classroom geography to create random constraints.	
	Use 'mantle of the expert'.	

How can I vary listening focus/voice?

Variety of focus can evoke a change in atmosphere, pace, create focus and stimulate renewed awareness of language and content.

Table 6.6 Varying listening

Opportunities	Behaviour	Opportunity
Vary listening focus/voice	Pupil voice	
	TA	
	Books on tape	
	Radio and podcasts	
	Community voices	

How can I address grammar in speech?

This is a tricky one and it's possible that school-wide policy has a role to play here. Addressing grammar in speech presupposes that pupils have the opportunity to speak and to practice making sense, out loud. Obviously, we do not necessarily speak in full sentences, we repeat ourselves, stop and start and use sounds to join one piece of speech to another when thinking about what we are to say next. Grammar in speech therefore does not automatically translate into writing. However, there are certain conventions that it is helpful to underpin. They might include tenses, plurals, and correct use of common prefixes and suffixes.

Table 6.7 Addressing grammar

Opportunities	Behaviour	Opportunity
Address grammar in speech by offering	Corrections	
	Explanations	
	Rewards	

How can I vary volume, tone and register?

Addressing tone, volume and register requires greater subtlety in consideration. If we take the easiest first it is helpful to think about how we use volume. We use it to indicate addressing the whole group, to communicate anger and to eliminate competition – or is there something more specific and more theatrical at play? Finding ways of cueing the class without volume of voice offers an interesting opportunity. We are trained to respond to the alert 'pings' on our phones, and to follow the 'fingers on lips' type hand signals in early years but seem to lose flexibility as children get older. Tone is a powerful tool, and one that can have a profound impact on the success of an interaction; while my preference is for an inquisitive tone as a default setting, the key is to model what you expect to promote.

Table 6.8 Varying volume

Opportunities	Behaviour	Opportunity
Vary volume, tone and register	Model appropriate tone and register.	
	Manage volume.	
	Identify inside, outside, individual and group voices.	

Thinking about resources

It's understandable to think of resources for differentiation as principally *material* resources: the provision of alternative books, reading schemes, worksheets, technology and equipment. These things come with a price tag and are relatively straightforward to quantify. Less so are the human resources involved in differentiation. This essential aspect of the inclusive classroom is much more difficult to capture. Bearing in mind that 70% of a typical school budget is spent on staff, finding ways to recognise and to manage the impact of making special educational provision on the time of teaching and support staff cannot be underestimated.

Why is resourcing for SEND an important consideration for teachers?

Funding for SEND is not ring fenced and therefore the agreed allocation of money with which to make special educational provision is notional within the school budget. While it is the responsibility of the Head and supervisory bodies to manage the overarching budgetary issues, it is in the interest of all parties to be clear about the cyclical nature of the principles underlying funding for SEND. They are as follows: define the learning difficulty (Assess) leading, agree on the SEN that result and the resources required (Plan), make the special educational provision (Do) and account for the impact (Review). In a political climate of austerity and shrinking school budgets it has never been more important to be able to triangulate the relationship between a pupil's learning difficulty, the resources required to make the necessary special educational provision, and the progress and attainment of children with SEND. If the provision fails to have an impact and pupils fail to meet the agreed expectations questions are likely to be raised as to the quality of teaching vs. the level of resourcing. Evidence that speaks to impact has implications for SEND resources and funding at all levels.

A classroom teacher necessarily has an important role to play in informing this process. It is teachers who manage classroom resources day to day – human, material and technological. Without the ability to feedback on the impact of the existing educational provision and the resources, making a useful contribution to the decision-making process is impossible.

How do I identify and explore the available resources?

Consider the different types of resources: human, material, technological and therapeutic. Details about provision to meet pupil's specific needs should be included in the SEN Information Report or the local offer. Consider the distinction between resources that are widely and consistently available to *all* members of the class and those resources that might be limited and used to support a struggling pupil – resources that might be considered 'additional to' and 'different from' the standard classroom offer. Without some notion of the distinction between resources which can be made available to all and those which are limited, it's hard to outline a special educational provision.

Use Table 6.9 as a guide to create an inventory of resources at your disposal. If you can do this with a colleague or your curricular team to create a shared pool of resources so much the better. Sharing this information across the school allows for greater clarity in terms of actual levels of resource and provides a useful supplement to existing provision mapping.

Table 6.9 Using resources

	Human	**Material**	**Technological**	**Therapeutic**
Standard	one-to-one support from teacher	Visual cues	Pen grips	
		Reading scheme supplementary work sheets	Wi-fi multimedia screen	
		Dry-wipe boards		
		Vocab lists		
Additional	one-to-one support LSA	Large-print books, manipulatives, visual cue cards,	Software for working memory mind-mapping	Small-group therapeutic
		Angled desks	Phonics	support by LSA
		Wobble cushions		Direct therapy

Don't forget to include centralised resources. While some material resources might be available in every classroom, it's not uncommon for schools to have centrally stored specialist materials designed to be shared across the staff, not least in the form of software licenses and the resources produced by colleagues. To avoid duplication, it's always a good idea to check with colleagues and the SENCO before you make or request to order a specific tool or material.

How do I audit the classroom environment in terms of visual cues?

Visual cues can be an essential resource for supporting working memory, recalling sequences, developing sight vocabulary and embedding a culture of self-help. These don't necessarily need to be ornate, permanent or time-consuming endeavours. A first step in augmenting or enhancing the visual cues available for pupils requiring support is to audit the existing environment. How useful is it in supporting learning?

In reference to a specific room in which you teach, complete the checklist of the visual cues available to pupils with learning difficulties (Table 6.10) and decide how they support access to teaching and learning.

Table 6.10 Visual cues audit

MR CHUFFI	
Effective teaching	**Visual cue**
Making links	Themed table featuring labelled items with curricular relevance
Risk taking	Lucky dip challenge box
Cognitive engagement	Quote of the week as a prompt to ongoing discussion
Higher-level thinking	Question of the week wall – children can post a question to test their teacher.
Checking **U**nderstanding	Interactive diagrams to illustrate key facts, games to check understanding
Frequent **F**eedback	Simple criteria and tools to aid self-assessment
Fostering **I**ndependence	Personal project feature display

It's clear that classroom walls serve both to celebrate achievement and offer an aide memoire to the journey. It's better to make informed and purposeful choices in the production of this visual environment than establish fixed conventions in maintaining it. It may be that displays change in nature and purpose or have a degree of regularity. The pupils are guides to what works.

Having surveyed literally hundreds of classrooms in the last four years, my view is that reductions in the visual feast on offer might be as effective as additions. Lengthy, stapled bundles of A4, covered with size 11 text, listing millions of 'helpful' criteria are the typical needle in the 'visual' haystack. They reveal more about a teacher's anxiety of omission than the pupil's joy of discovery.

What might pupils usefully do to create their own visual cues?

The creation of visual cues is not only the province of the teacher or TA. Making a Low-Tech Toolkit for pupils to use independently builds self-awareness and is a low-cost route to engagement in learning.

Suggested items for your Low Tech Tool Kit

Illustration 6.2 Create a low-tech toolkit

Source: James Gray

The kit consists of a plastic folder containing a few basic items: sticky notes, plastic sticky tabs, colours markers of any kind, a key ring holding a mini-colour coded time table, a laminated dry-wipe card, a manipulative toy and basic writing equipment. The kit can offer all pupils an opportunity to personalise the learning experience and better manage their own needs.

The multi-sensory opportunities afforded by a few simple items of stationary, thoughtfully utilised, are endless when it comes to tackling the impact of the core deficits (working memory, phonological processing and processing time) which I touched upon earlier. Each item can be used to manage learning more actively and can add appeal to a pupil requiring a higher level of sensory feedback. They enable a proactive approach and can help a pupil to keep things in mind, to specify and identify information or to flag a problem or error without permanently defacing the book or work produced. They also offer a very real smorgasbord of opportunities to encouraging a pupil to develop their own strategies in managing their own learning.

Training activity

1 This is most useful when done in a pair or small group.
2 Choose a common lesson topic or familiar activity.
3 Take one item at a time from the kit.
4 Think of a way to use the item as a visual cue to support a pupil in engaging in the MR CHUFFI agenda (e.g. sticky note).

Examples might include:

- **Making links.** Pupil uses the note to flag a prior piece of learning in the pupil's book/file connected to today's lesson.
- **Risk taking.** Pupils find, flag and copy an unfamiliar word from a text and try to work out and record on back the correct meaning of each one – following checking using a dictionary. New words can be stuck in to vocab record and returned to in future sessions or at home.

Thinking about grouping

The purview of this section is confined to the daily, incidental grouping considerations that can be made by a classroom teacher. Whether the school or department creates groups configured into mixed ability, sets or streams it is likely that pupils with SpLDs needs are likely to be represented across the ability range. Unfortunately, specialist advice – while often concerned with establishing a peer group – is less helpful in regard to grouping in relation to ability and rarely addresses group dynamics. Often the child with learning difficulties is assumed to be best served by specific positioning: near the source material, at the front of the classroom or close to the teacher. This can translate into social isolation of one type of another. While it may be vital for some children to have access to a specific facility or technology it's also important that routines incorporate a degree of flexibility. A situation where a child's learning difficulty confines them to sit in the same seat, or with the same person, for the duration of their learning experience singles them out as different and is to be avoided. If a child is to be included in the mainstream learning experience, a social experience of learning with other pupils forms an important part of that.

The audit that follows in Table 6.11 offers an opportunity to consider how your existing decisions and practice supports access to a diverse group-dynamic for pupils with learning difficulties. The audit can be adapted to use as a tool for the following: recording and/or reflection; to help you to keep tabs on group-based learning opportunities; and identifying the focus and the impact a change in grouping might have on the learning and attainment of those involved.

How can I assign groups?

Exploring variations can help to create a variety of grouping routines with which pupils can become familiar allowing an explicit link to be made between the social aspect of learning and clear expectations about social behaviour and outcome.

Table 6.11 Grouping

	Method of selection	Frequency	Rationale/Impact
Random groups	Lolly sticks with names	Date	M
	Apps – group sort	Tally	R
	Picking colour coded pom-poms	Names	C
	Deck of cards – suits numbers etc.		H
	Birthday months – Q and A		U
			FF
			I
Student selected	Friendship groups		M
	Find person doing same task		R

	Method of selection	Frequency	Rationale/Impact
	Agreeing roles		C
	New person each lesson		H
			U
			FF
			I
Teacher selected	Alphabetical		M
	Neighbour		R
	Day of week		C
	Ability		H
	Time of day		U
	Teams		FF
			I

Thinking about outcome

The notion of differentiation by outcome at one time came to be synonymous with refraining from making any adaptation to teaching but accepting the variations in terms of the quality of work produced. Differentiation by outcome to some extent was an educational oxymoron. An exam is a prime example of differentiation by outcome: everyone does the same task, in the same context and the outcome varies.

However, there is a form of differentiation by outcome that can indeed offer pupils with learning difficulties an opportunity to use their diversity of skills and thinking. It relies upon the teacher's ability to specify the aim of the lesson in such a way that form and process can vary. A teacher needs a lesson plan that lends itself to showing understanding or skill rather than one requiring recall and repetition of a specific process. While it is now more common practice for pupils to select tasks with various levels of challenge (more of that in 'Thinking about task'), it's less common for pupils to be able to select the mode of their response to a single problem or challenge.

Building in the possibility of variation, in terms of communicating knowledge and understanding, can be a lifeline for pupils who struggle with any number of challenges from auditory memory to literacy or fine motor-skills. Children with learning difficulties might take up to four times as long as their peers to write a well-crafted paragraph; the conventions of a handwritten response are so laborious that they often constrain thought and limit memory rather than give it structure. Simply teaching a pupil to touch type and to use a laptop can be transformative, producing legible writing that can be manipulated and re-presented as necessary deals with many auditory and working memory issues. These pupils require the teacher to at least ask the question: Is it possible to show the same knowledge and understanding in a different way, perhaps with flow chart, a model, an oral assessment, a movie trailer, a presentation, a collage or a cartoon?

Unless the task is specifically about process, the aim of all assignments is that the pupil engages with the material and think about it. Building in choice in terms of outcome can do much to facilitate that process and allow the pupil to pursue media and modes of interaction that may be more accessible to them. In this way differentiation by outcome can offer pupils with learning difficulties the opportunity to approach a challenge from a position of strength.

Thinking about pace

Delay in processing time affects the majority of pupils with learning difficulties; therefore, a flexible approach to the pace of learning must play a part in good habits for differentiation.

There are four aspects to consider.

What about the pace of speech?

It's vital to for teachers to be aware of their pace of speech when introducing, discussing and instructing. Teachers are often confident speakers who use language with ease and enthusiasm. It is easy to overlook the impact of poor auditory processing, memory and receptive language difficulties experienced by a pupil with a SpLD. These pupils may well have difficulty in identifying the important information from a continuous stream of teacher talk comprised of explanations, instructions, details, questions, jokes and asides. In the same way that people often re-read a page of dense text to decipher its meaning, a pupil who struggles with auditory processing or memory may need the same kind of opportunity to address spoken information. It is also likely that they may not have mastered the necessary oracy to help themselves by interjecting to ask for repetitions or clearer information.

This places the responsibility on teachers to be aware of their pace of speech and to recognise that less is sometimes more. It's important to check assumptions regarding a pupil's recall and understanding of information covered orally. A lack of either is often construed as 'not listening' when actually is more to do with a lack of ability to process the volume and complexity of what has been said.

What about the pace of processing?

It's essential to recognise that a pupil with learning difficulties might need additional time to process the material with which they are presented, from a simple instruction to a new concept. Finding ways to build in and to structure thinking time can compensate for this problem. Fostering a cognitively engaged class requires specific opportunities for critical thinking, reflection and questioning; there is no reason why a pupil with processing delay cannot be included in the 'thinking classroom', actively engaged in working together with their peers to explore what is being learned. A metacognitive approach where pupils are encouraged to question their own knowledge can be an essential and productive use of time. Offering a range of activities that might centre around an open question affords a genuine opportunity, in a low-stress context, for the pupil with learning difficulties to question, to process and to consider a response whether tackled in a group or as an individual.

What about the pace of the curriculum?

Specifically varying the pace of a single lesson to reduce, omit or even to augment an aspect of the curriculum is a more contentious area for the time-pressured mainstream classroom.

There are always likely to be pupils working at different levels of attainment, including below, at or above age-related expectations. In primary schools, it's not unusual for teachers to acknowledge the need for pupils to be working on material relevant to levels of proficiency, specifically in core areas like numeracy and literacy (more of that in the 'Thinking about task' section). However, making specific curricular accommodations is more complex in a larger secondary setting where the pace of learning is ostensibly controlled by setting and schedules for public examinations.

Any discussion about curricular pace is incomplete without reference to the Mastery agenda, especially in regard to mathematic teaching. Its central principles relate to having high expectations of all pupils while providing opportunities for pupils who grasp knowledge and skills quickly to deepen their knowledge and understanding rather than to move on the next topic. In this way, pacing the curriculum to focus on proficiency and depth is a prerequisite for advancement and development. While it contrasts in many ways to the small-group, skill-based, overlearning approach to teaching of mathematical concepts which is often used in supporting pupils with SpLD, it shares the principle of encouraging pupils to work at different levels and at different paces towards the learning objective. Another interesting similarity is the apparent relevance of the small-group setting; as the evidence on Mastery suggests[5] the approach has proved most effective in improving the achievement of pupils when they worked in groups, with some peer support, rather than entirely independently.

It's widely accepted that pupils require a flexible and proficiency-based approach to literacy and numeracy skills, which often form the focus for programmes of additional support and intervention. However, this proficiency model does not generally extend to the broader curriculum, which continues to gain in pace and complexity as each school year passes. While the law protects the right of children with learning difficulties to a 'broad and balanced' and most often 'mainstream' curriculum, this also creates a tension between the momentum of said curriculum and the slow or uneven development of skills underpinning independent learning. In attempting to compensate for deficits by providing support for literacy and numeracy while children continue to progress through the rest of the curriculum, schools can generate some cumbersome and counter-intuitive practices. Finding space to work at the pupil's pace can create curricular conflicts and omissions that can be left to the pupil to resolve.

Common practice in USA, France, Germany and Spain, aimed at resolving the tension described earlier, is for pupils to be held back and to repeat a year if they fail to achieve a specific level of proficiency and attainment. While in Britain this approach is not entirely uncommon in the independent sector, it's virtually unheard of in the state sector and remains deeply unpopular with educators. Parents would appear to disagree judging from a 2012 YouGov survey identifying that 61% of parents with school-age children support holding children back a year if necessary.[6]

Funding structures and performance indicators for schools are so closely tied to age-related milestones that it's hard to find much room for personalisation in terms of the curriculum from Key Stage 1 to 3. That being said, simply being aware of the fact that a pupil is coping with additional lessons or therapeutic sessions, alongside the existing curriculum, can help. Class teachers can thereby make explicit exceptions and/or agreements about how to adapt expectations for class and homework. Bearing in mind that the pupil is unlikely to be responsible for the inconvenience of alternative arrangements can help to avoid the conflict, frustration and stress that sometimes are the result.

What about time for repetition?

Pupils with learning difficulties often need to return to concepts repeatedly after explicit teaching is completed. Recall may not necessarily work predictably and assuming steady and cumulative knowledge building is likely to result in disappointment and sometimes disagreement. It is not uncommon for pupils with SpLDs to work with focus, to have shown their understanding and their ability to apply knowledge, and then subsequently to struggle to repeat the process particularly in a different context or while under duress. Overlearning, repetition and the active exploration of the transfer of knowledge into different contexts is an essential part of a differentiated approach to pace. It's necessary to prepare for the frustration for both pupils and teachers that results from the extremes of good days and bad days. Returning to the subject, talking about the learning experience itself, making the links of where and how it is likely to be useful or relevant supports the formation of a longer-term memory, a more successful relationship and a realistic approach to progress.

Thinking about task

This might seem the most obvious route to differentiation. To differentiate by task is to run the classroom by creating a series of subgroups where individual pupils or small groups are engaged in different work.

This kind of approach can be most effective when highly individualised and skills related, for example by use of a structured reading comprehension scheme or online tailored numeracy programme where the point of entry is determined by progress to date through a prescribed set of materials. It offers the teacher an opportunity to use a differentiation strategy, as it has the advantage of being self-recording and easily observed, operating within existing linear assessment criteria.

This model is to be found in mainstream classrooms across the curriculum; pupils are offered a version of the colour-coded task, covertly calibrated to a level of 'ability'. Teachers or pupils themselves select the 'level' of work to be attempted, making a judgement based on prior attainment and most often the teacher's appreciation of the degree of challenge. Whether the system pertains to classroom work, extension tasks or homework this direct approach to differentiation can be appealing in that it appears to tick both the access and personalisation boxes. However, a system that relies on a generic notion of ability has some serious limitations for the child with learning difficulties in that it illustrates and rehearses the misguided notion that learning exists within a straightforward hierarchy of easy, harder and difficult – and sitting alongside those descriptors are the complimentary value judgements of good, better and best.

The profile of strengths and weaknesses represented by these children is such that the nature of challenge is individual. Having regard to the load that a task might place on working memory, processing time, phonological skills and executive function acknowledges the specifics of the challenge and helps to characterise it more accurately.

Most tasks will present an augmented challenge in some form for pupils with SpLD and affect one or all of the following: access to the information required to consider a proposition, reasoning with said proposition or undertaking the necessary process to correctly record their response.

It is important for the teacher to remember the characteristic, uneven nature of the cognitive profile of SpLD pupils. A phonological difficulty is not necessarily a semantic one, a fine motor problem leading to poorly presented work is not automatically indicative of poor non-verbal reasoning and great spelling is no guarantee of age-appropriate comprehension. These observations would suggest that differentiation by means of a simple task hierarchy is likely to miss more marks than it hits.

Pupils with learning difficulties, like their neurotypical peers, require tasks that ignite their intellectual curiosity and challenge them to explore a subject rather than tasks which offer repeated public opportunities to showcase their deficits in the name of closing the skills gap. If inclusion is to have any meaning and purpose, inherent in anything we ask pupils to do should be an invitation to engage cognitively with the subject and to participate in the thinking. Therefore, unless the differentiated task has been created specifically to develop or short cut according to individual strengths or weaknesses, there is more to be gained from encouraging pupils to attempt the same tasks but with encouragement and opportunities to establish additional personal tools or strategies they might need in order to reach the objective.

Watching a pupil with a SpLD desperately trying to emulate the process and efforts of their neurotypical peers is rather like watching a cyclist pedal furiously up a hill in a low gear while a competitor sails passed, with far less effort, in a higher one. They both may get there in the end but the child with the learning difficulty is so exhausted that they look for a flat route for the rest of the day. Variations to task should diversify the route into and through challenge rather than simply offering a longer or a shorter path to demonstrating their existing knowledge or skills. Instead of differentiating the number, style and sophistication of questions we need to think more about how many ways it is possible to arrive at answers and how many ways it might be possible to present those answers. This involves disentangling the process from the desired outcome and identifying the essential elements and those which are flexible.

Planning in this way requires the identification of both the learning opportunities and the potential pitfalls of classroom activities, locating the stumbling blocks. Shifting the focus from process to outcome can be a more powerful motivator to engage with learning than the offer of a highly structured and scaffolded activity. It helps to ensure that any learning objective shared successfully encapsulates the rationale and aim of the work to be undertaken, and recalling the bigger picture, rather than simply listing the tasks to be completed.

This approach requires clarity of purpose on the part of teachers in setting aspirations and expectations of pupils with learning difficulties. David Didau talks eloquently about 'the dark art of differentiation' in his book *What if everything you knew about differentiation was wrong?* (Didau, 2016) While he is speaking to mainstream pupils he makes an important point which in my experience translates directly for pupils with learning difficulties, namely that all children have a right to find themselves at the edges and to 'struggle no matter what their ability'(Didau, 2016, p. 320). Having equally high expectations of all pupils, despite identified barriers to learning, is the common denominator in terms of well-differentiated tasks.

As a quick self-help checklist, when differentiating tasks, aim for tasks that are:

- specific and personalised, building on strengths and emphasizing progression;
- designed to access the MR CHUFFI agenda;
- designed to build self-awareness and resilience rather than self-consciousness and dependency; and
- developmental and use a support toolbox.

Try to avoid:

- systems that enable less-confident pupils to choose something 'simple' and to remain within their comfort zone;
- systems that reinforce unhelpful assumptions and beliefs about ability across curricula; and
- practices that can lead to unhelpful direct comparisons between peers and lead to loss of self-esteem.

Thinking about assessment

When I looked up the word 'assessment' in my father's old Oxford English Dictionary I found, to my surprise, that all of the references pertained to taxation. In 1933 it appears the word assessment referred exclusively to the estimation of the value of property. In the 21st-century assessment is everywhere and describes any number of value ascribing processes from intelligence testing to eligibility for social security. It's the processes of assessment that give education its currency and determines the worth of knowledge and understanding.

In order to think about how best to approach this process for pupils with learning difficulties it's worth considering some basic facts about life after education. Principally, that beyond the school gates, all young people face the same competitive, economic reality. The measures that exist in school to level the playing field and to consider disadvantage effectively cease to exist. The free market economy is not concerned with how far a student has travelled, as long as they arrive at the required destination.

The questions are not what can be done to differentiate assessment for pupils with learning difficulties but how to use assessment most effectively to prepare children for a successful future and how to ensure that teachers recognise and optimise the impact of the messages they send to pupils about the value of their work.

In terms of recognising the impact of the message, it's worth remembering that we all carry somewhere a memory of the classroom. Usually a moment of deep pride or deeper consternation. Teachers provide children with their first experience of professional judgement; the teacher is the first 'expert' they encounter, the first figure of authority outside of the family. Words carry weight, especially for Generation Z, growing up in a society addicted to snap judgements and instant expressions of approval or disapproval. Young people are so bombarded by trite and empty examples of winners and losers, why wouldn't they apply the same binary logic to themselves and our assessments of them? This finds its iteration everywhere; in the accrual of 'follows', 'likes' and 'retweets' on social media, the steady stream of reality shows promoting the power of a gladiatorial 'thumbs up' or 'thumbs down' or even in the binary opposition represented by the 'in' or 'out' votes cast in recent referenda.

In some ways assessment might be considered a subject over which individual teachers have limited control. A series of fixed points to measure and note. After all, it's likely that a school has an explicit marking policy and a reporting schedule which requires adherence to an established timescale and prescribes a format for providing feedback to students and their families. However, the approach we take to assessment can offer a powerful opportunity to subvert this binary narrative of winners and losers, which is so damaging to children with learning difficulties, and help us to cultivate balance, self-knowledge, confidence and skill in terms of discerning one's own ability and exploring opportunity.

How do I make assessment work for children with learning difficulties?

- Provide accurate and useful formative and summative feedback.
- Make specific concessions for examinations and tests.
- Collect and use diagnostic information.
- Consider motivation.

How do I provide accurate and useful formative and summative feedback?

The quality and frequency of feedback is repeatedly cited in educational research as an intrinsic component of effective teaching and the resultant pupil progress. Frequent Feedback is a key part of the MR CHUFFI agenda. A 2016 report, 'Eliminating unnecessary workload around marking', recommended that marking should be 'meaningful, manageable and motivating' (Independent Teacher Workload Review Group, 2016, p. 5). Despite a scarcity of specific research, highlighted in the 2016 EEF Marking Review, it's hard to see a model of teaching now or in the future that does not contain mandatory regular feedback from teacher to pupil.

While much has been written to define and explore formative and summative feedback, the practical realities of these two processes can pose problems for the child with learning difficulties and are worth additional consideration.

How do I make feedback meaningful and manageable?

Formative assessment should contribute to learning and influence the outcome recorded in the summative assessment; in written and oral form it should both facilitate and record the learning conversation.

Figure 6.1 outlines potential issues in terms of access to written and oral formative feedback for pupils with learning difficulties.

Feedback	Opportunities	Barriers
Oral	contextual	Public exposure
	Immediate – before misunderstandings develop	Processing time
	Dialogue/questions	Auditory Memory remembering what has been said
		Mixed messages (TA vs Teacher)
Written	Permanent	Reading ability
	Accessible to all readers	Complexity
	Record of progress and interaction	Lack of opportunity for questioning
	Focused	

Figure 6.1 Barriers to engagement with feedback

How can I address the barriers to access and engagement with feedback?

While pupils with learning difficulties may fully engage in oral feedback and take an active part in discussions about learning, there may be real difficulties in terms of recall for all the reasons outlines earlier and covered in the 'Thinking about dialogue' section. Simply converting everything into written form presents problems too; I have yet to meet a pupil who enjoys opening their book to find half a page of notes from their teacher, in any colour. Pride and ownership are things to promote and to balance against advice and marking.

Thankfully technology affords us both low and high-tech means for creating a semi-permanent set of possibilities for feedback, thus addressing gaps, omissions and corrections that can prompt recall while promoting self-esteem.

Removable tabs and post-it notes can be used by teachers, LSA and pupils to indicate concerns, to communicate and to underpin the metacognitive processes of learning. Unlike marking in pen and notes in the planner, they can be removed, keeping work 'clean' (and kept as a record if necessary or desirable) but serving to flag difficulties as they arise, indicating confusions and questions on the part of the pupil or teacher. Sticky notes and tabs can support the recording and recall of oral feedback without the need for lengthy narrative, while providing the flexibility to returning to an issue at subsequent opportunity. They can be used in the textbook, workbook, folder or diary to review, to sort or to question any content – from flagging the correct page for homework to tracking key words, identifying target phonemes, reviewing concepts, correcting spelling, learning formulae, highlighting gaps and making suggestions.

These methods are almost universally applicable in every subject, offering the opportunity to create codes of communication and aides to memory via simple colour and shape codes or augmented with symbols, dates or annotation.

These semi-permanent feedback tools have the additional advantage of facilitating an ongoing conversation with the pupil which can include support staff, therapeutic specialists or parents without additional administrative difficulty or replication.

High-tech solutions

Using a laptop or a tablet to complete work and to interact with staff offers all the utility of the more of low-tech solutions discussed earlier. To work effectively a number of practical hurdles must first be overcome:

- consistent access to a machine that works and that can link to networks, printers and Wi-Fi;
- a machine that is safe and easy to transport to and from school;
- pupil cooperation (if using a laptop singles a pupil out as different it's quite possible they might choose to struggle on without it rather than be seen to be treated differently).

A laptop allows for access to Microsoft Innovative Educator or Google Educator, offering a huge range of teacher–pupil interactivity including:

- video and audio commentary (e.g., a PowerPoint Mix – facilitating a conversation or thorough commentary);

- use of the Word Review pane; and
- direct message/email contact.

Summative feedback

Summative feedback serves to demonstrate the extent to which the pupil has met a set of criteria. It's clear from earlier chapters that establishing a baseline and assessing performance and attainment against norms is a fundamental and underpinning principle of effective provision for pupils with learning difficulties. It's crucial that teachers offer feedback with a clear understanding of the pupil's current level of ability, across the range of skills. If this individual consideration is overlooked it's impossible to discern effectively if a pupil is working at, or near, the edge of that ability. Summative feedback that simply refers to the pupil's relationship to an 'age-appropriate' group standard can become punitive, demotivating and focused on areas of underachievement rather acknowledging of hard work and incremental progress made.

Without some additional thought, the constant assessments and judgements that exist to measure performance – especially now that schools generally consider performance in terms of age-related expectations – can leave pupils with learning difficulties feeling anxious, embarrassed, frustrated and demotivated.

How do I make formative and summative feedback motivating?

Securing and maintaining the motivation of pupils with learning difficulties is perhaps the biggest challenge of all. Meaningful and manageable systems of feedback need also to promote motivation to engage with the process and struggle of learning.

Twelve years in a specialist environment gave me plenty of opportunity to meet 11 years olds with their self-esteem in tatters, having experienced wave after wave of entirely negative feedback. Unfortunately, it is still not unheard of for children with diagnosed learning difficulties to be told repeatedly that they are lazy and careless, to see their work ripped up and thrown away, to be asked to repeat tasks over breaks and to be reprimanded for producing work that is entirely consistent with their identified levels of ability, as if somehow they can be shamed into improving their skills.

Adults quickly assert their power to avoid tasks they find miserable. I'd go to almost any length to avoid ironing, reverse parking, making clothes, assembling flat pack furniture and packing suitcases – spatial awareness not being my strong suite. My repeated failure to do these things without support felt both irritating and exposing. Thankfully, it's been possible to trade skills with friends and family and to negotiate a way out of pretty much all of the above (and more!). However, there are things that 21st-century life, and certainly 21st-century schooling, makes it impossible to avoid – reading, writing and number being three. If I was faced with days full of the tasks with which I struggle most, when even increased exposure and help only slightly improved my skills, aware that I could barely cope while my peers achieved proficiency, I imagine I'd be miserable or rebellious or both.

UK school hours are long. OECD Statistics for 2014 showed that in the UK pupils spent just under 8 000 hours on their primary and lower secondary curriculum schooling.

That's more than Germany, Japan, Sweden, Belgium and Italy – more than half of the OECD members in fact (OECD, 2014). The same report indicated that reading, writing, literature and mathematics take up more than a quarter of that instruction time notwithstanding that language, communication and literacy skills are intrinsic across the curriculum.

Given the level of challenge, how do we motivate pupils to take on board our advice and to persevere, especially when opportunities to close the gaps with neurotypical peers take the form of lunchtime sessions, before and after school reading clubs, and study groups that remove them from possible more appealing options. The 'more is better' approach to curriculum planning results in days given over to an even greater proportion of skills teaching than their more-proficient peers.

Carol Dweck, the psychologist, author and TED speaker, introduced the world to the notion of *Mindset* (Dweck, 2017). Her research into the impact of specific forms of praise on American school children has identified how powerful and limiting it can be to hold a fixed notion of intellectual ability rather than to promote and foster a 'growth mindset'. Her work asserts that children should be encouraged to understand the positive correlation between effort and outcome, while identifying that to be useful feedback has also to be realistic. Where a criterion for success has not been met, a competition lost, or an exam failed, the key phrase to add to the message is 'not yet', acknowledging both the current reality while still implying future achievement.

Dweck tells us that praise should identify strengths in the learning process, the effort and application made by the student rather than to offer congratulation for talent and intelligence as innate qualities.

While Dweck's studies prove the success of the approach in disadvantaged and vulnerable communities, specific studies with pupils with diagnosed learning difficulties have been limited but encouragingly successful. Applying this approach to feedback for pupils with identified learning difficulties is an interesting proposition. My own experience as a special school Head tells me that mindset matters for all pupils, especially those with learning difficulties. A core principle was to assume that it was for the school to provide education in such a way that all pupils would achieve better outcomes than those predicted by our baseline tools; our aim was not to meet those expectations but to exceed them. We planned for our alumni to face the same choices as all other school leavers; to progress to further education and beyond to higher education or a meaningful vocational course of study, apprenticeship or fulfilling career. Pupils and teachers aspired to achievements that result from real choice, self-confidence and self-knowledge. The absolute belief in the possibility of growth, the 'when' and not the 'if', ran like Brighton Rock through every aspect of provision.

The mantra of 'high challenge, low stress' can be actively promoted by all school systems including feedback that refers constantly to the bigger picture, linking short and longer-term goals. Look to minimise time spent on issues of compliance and procedural idiosyncrasy that dog pupils with poor short-term auditory memory. Assessment requires routine and consistency rather than fussy formality; in short, make compliance easy, make spare equipment available, and respond to disorganisation as calmly as possible so that energy goes into intellectual effort and not excuses.

What are the considerations to be made in terms of tests and examinations?

Assessment schedules tend to be led by fixed points, like public exams and staff time-tables; the operational necessities tend to outweigh other considerations. Recognising the implications of test and examination schedules for pupils with learning difficulties is essential in order to strike a balance between the dual purpose of measuring knowledge and understanding and preparation for performing independently and under pressure.

While public exams create absolute constraints, mindful planning in regard to school based-assessments can take account of the following.

Timing

Finding the flexibility to avoid clashes and overload is always in the interest of the pupil with learning difficulties. Whether in the form of end-of-module tests or school exams, finding ways to acknowledge and to break up the workload does something to mitigate the intensity and to encourage fuller participation in the actual intellectual process.

Sharing information with colleagues in advance about class-based testing and assess-ment points can help to the overload that is sometimes needlessly created when different kinds of assessments coincide.

Additional time is one of the most widely used access arrangements available for pupils with learning difficulties; however, this arrangement can be used to positive effect only when the pupil has had an opportunity to think through with their teachers the best ways to utilise this additional time and to practice using it. The additional time can create more problems than it solves if its impact is not properly calculated. Problems arise if it either concertinas one paper against the next in a relentless chain or gets added to the beginning of exams and thereby identifies a deeply self-conscious minority of pupils who are invited to begin while other pupils sit, wait and watch. Both are more common practices than one would expect.

How do I help to manage pupil anxiety?

It is no surprise to anyone involved in education that mental health, specifically levels of anxiety, amongst school children have never been higher. Anxiety and its effect on learning are well documented but often underestimated or overlooked. The mental health char-ity Young Minds estimates that one in six children and young people will experience an anxiety-related problem. Neuroscience, common sense and experience tells us that it is virtually impossible to learn and indeed to engage higher-level thinking while the brain is experiencing the effects of adrenalin; fight and flight responses controlled by the sympa-thetic nervous system take over relegating conscious action. In his book *Dyslexia and men-tal health*, Neil Alexander Passe looks at features of stress and anxiety common to children with the SpLD dyslexia (Alexander-Passe, 2015). He makes the point that as a situation is perceived as too challenging it provokes an unpleasant and unmanageable stress response which can then make future, similar events the source of anxiety. Recognising the disabling effects of anxiety and acknowledging just how difficult it might be for a pupil to express the need for help is a significant challenge for teachers. While anxiety can manifest as nail-biting, poor sleep and tearfulness, it may as frequently manifest in withdrawal, avoidance or refusal to participate.

Clearly, the classroom is not a therapeutic space where individual problems can be worked through to resolution. However, there are things we can do to avoid placing additional stress on pupils at exam time, thus creating a safe, purposeful and supportive atmosphere:

- offer pupils clear and timely information in advance about assessment;
- be as explicit as possible about the content to be tested;
- explain how the test will work (is it in the usual room, are the desks in their usual spaces, is there a time limit and how will it be indicated?);
- make sure rules for communication with peers are explicit;
- if possible have a practice run so that pupils can get used the format of the process and the paper;
- look at the test format together (this avoids confusion in the face of a rubric, page numbers and instruction about blank pages, caps or lower case, marking scheme in brackets, signatures etc.);
- make sure they know if they can ask you a question and how;
- have some clear pointers as to what they can do if they get worried, stuck or finish early; and
- have manipulatives to hand and spare equipment on offer.

Sharing results

Finding ways to avoid direct comparisons in terms of attainment between pupils is not easy. Nature loves a hierarchy. However, it is possible to be considerate and to avoid practices which might add to a child's concerns. Results do not need to be shared in public; they don't need to be posted or read out. They can be shared individually, in small groups, by support staff or at different times and with sufficient context to identify progress and new goals.

What are the considerations to be made in terms of specialist assessments?

Pupils with learning difficulties are likely to be exposed to a more rigorous regime of assessment and testing than other pupils. One-to-one assessments by psychologists and therapists can become part and parcel of life. The intensely analytical process that identifies and describes learning difficulties, specific or otherwise, can have a lasting and positive effect when the product is put to good use but should not be underestimated as source of great anxiety before, during and after administration. While these considerations will generally need to be made by the SENCO it's important for classroom teachers to be aware of the process:

Preparation: The pupil and the family must be consulted and have an opportunity to consider the reasons for referral, the experience itself and the opportunity it represents and give their permission for the assessment.

Environment: One-to-one assessments can take place onsite, in a private space or indeed in an offsite centre or in the home, avoiding interruptions, noise and distractions.

Timing: Assessments should be planned well in advance and arranged sensitively. Avoid removing pupils from the middle of a lesson or returning them to one after having endured hours of intensive observation and testing.

Feedback: The report itself can be a dense document, full of numerical, technical and specialist language. It always requires discussion and should be a prompt to meet those involved in referral. The pupil and their family are a central part of this process.

Sharing: The recommendations of the report are likely to contain advice that is relevant to teaching staff and those responsible for the child's curriculum. While it's clear that this advice should be shared, the specifics of how and where and with whom should be carefully considered. Corridors, offices with doors open to public spaces, the canteen and sometimes the staff room itself are not appropriate spaces for such discussions.

Storage: These reports are highly sensitive documents often containing detailed personal, family and medical histories. They cannot ever be left in public view, on open screens or on desks where pupils, other parents or visitors might access them.

Self-evaluation

What were the key messages from this chapter?

What do I need to review?

Which activities have I tried?

Which activities would I like to try?

Things I'd like to know more about:

Is this chapter relevant to a specific situation, pupil or class?

Notes

1 The Communication Trust Website, Youth Justice Programme website: www.thecommunicationtrust.org. uk/projects/youth-justice/
2 To view a model for effective listening, see https://teachingcommons.stanford.edu/resources/teaching/ student-teacher-communication/characteristics-effective-listening. Also see Bergquist and Phillips (1977, p. 207).
3 Let's Talk Makaton, Website: www.makaton.org/training/findTraining?gclid=EAIaIQobChMIjMj w0K_m1wlV4b_tCh39dQOhEAAYASAAEgICKvD_BwE
4 *The Guardian Online UK*, 'Screen time guidelines need to be built on evidence, not hype', Open Letter, January 2017. See www.theguardian.com/science/head-quarters/2017/jan/06/screen-time-guidelines-need-to-be-built-on-evidence-not-hype
5 The Education Endowment Foundation Website, Evidence Summaries: https://educationendowmentfoundation.org.uk/evidence-summaries/teaching-learning-toolkit/mastery-learning/
6 Bonnie Gardiner and Hannah Thompson, YouGov UK Website: https://yougov.co.uk/news/2012/04/27/ holding-pupils-back-year/

Chapter 7

How can I work most effectively with Teaching Assistants?

This chapter considers how teachers can work with Teaching Assistants (TAs) in their classrooms to support the learning of pupils with SpLDs most effectively. It sets out the size of the resource represented by TAs and examines the research into their effectiveness and impact.

In looking at their potential role in supporting effective approaches to differentiated teaching. The chapter examines how the DR GOPTA and MR CHUFFI agendas can offer support and structure to underpin the contribution of TAs with a view to optimising the impact for the pupil.

The chapter closes in considering how TAs can make a unique cross curricular contribution to effective differentiation, identification and monitoring. The chapter concludes with consideration of how TAs can use the tools presented in this and other sections of the book to co-ordinate their efforts with class teachers and ensure a consistent experience for the pupils they support.

What do I need to know about TAs?

TAs represent more than a quarter of the school workforce. In November 2016 there were 957, 900 full-time equivalent (FTE) school workforce employees, 28% of that workforce were TAs. Numbers of FTE TAs has risen overall since the introduction of the School Workforce Census in 2010, when there were just over 218,000 FTE TAs to more than 265,000 in 2016. This FTE represents a workforce of more than 387,000 full-time and part-time staff. Between 2015 and 2016 while the total number of TAs rose overall, the numbers in the secondary sector fell by 4.2%, leaving 50,100 FTE in secondary schools and 174,500 in primary schools (DFE, 2016b).

Considering the huge financial investment represented by a workforce of such size and complexity, the role of TAs and their impact on pupils' learning outcomes has been under particular scrutiny for some time.

What impact do TAs have on pupil outcomes?

In 2009 the Institute of Education and partners produced a report entitled 'The Deployment and Impact of Support Staff' (DISS) which analysed the impact of all support staff and in particular the effect of TAs on pupil outcomes. Its findings highlighted a number of concerns about the deployment, training and impact of teaching assistants used to support pupils including those with Special Educational Needs (SEN) across both primary and secondary settings. The result of this model of support was found to have a 'systematic' negative effect on progress in English, mathematics and science for pupils across all year groups and a negative effect in terms of reduced teacher-to-pupil interaction. The model of practice was found to be reactive, task-focused and one that was likely to 'close down' rather than open up learning conversations with pupils.

There followed a report entitled 'Making Best Use of Teaching Assistants' (MITA) (Sharples, et al., 2015) produced by the Educational Endowment Foundation in 2015, authored by Blatchford, Webster and Sharples (the first two authors were both involved in the production of the previous DISS report; Blatchford, et al., 2008), went on to make seven recommendations about the most effective use of TAs. The authors' recommendations for TA practice were divided into three categories: working in classrooms, in one-to-one or small-group settings and in making relevant connections between the two.

TAs make up a significant proportion of the school workforce.

Successive recent studies have raised questions about the impact of TAs on pupil progress.

What is the best practice model for TAs?

The guidance recommended that TAs should be properly trained for their role in classrooms and sufficiently prepared to support and supplement teaching, enabling the teacher–pupil relationship rather than replacing it. In doing this they should encourage pupils to take ownership of their work and develop the skills to tackle it independently. The DISS Report advised against the use of TAs in providing informal support for pupils with low attainment. When providing targeted support in small groups or one-to-one support the recommendation was that TAs be trained to deliver specific, evidence-based interventions and take a role in helping pupils involved to make connections between the interventions and their independent classroom work.

Recommendations for best practice suggest TAs should enable the teacher–pupil relationship and support pupils in making links and developing independence

Recommendations for best practice suggest TAs are effective when delivering specific interventions.

What gets in the way of best practice?

The DISS found that TAs were highly valued by teachers, having a positive impact on the atmosphere and management of the classroom and in terms of teacher workload. However, this was not found to translate into best practice regarding habits for teaching and learning and successful pupil outcomes.

Lack of definition in terms of TA and LSA roles: Often TAs and LSAs have unique or idiosyncratic job descriptions that fail to identify key aims common to all. If there are key differences between support staff working in class, it's in the interest of all concerned to identify and clarify how those differences are designed to advantage the pupils. Further it is worth being aware of the extent to which those differences are consistent with features of practice.

Lack of training and preparation: One of the most significant impediments to more effective working practice for TAs was found to be their lack of preparedness for a specific role in lessons. This seems to include deficiencies in terms of subject knowledge, training in SEN or learning difficulties, and an overwhelmingly idiosyncratic and ad hoc approach to communication about support when time does become available. Unfortunately, effective communication is not as straightforward as simply finding time to talk as the communication around the specifics of support as well as being sporadic, anecdotal or chronological is more often than not outside of a common theoretical framework. The limitations placed on this process by workload (and often by issues of working hours which can often exclude TAs from non-contact time and the training schedule) makes it necessary for there to be a shared understanding about the structure of the conversations to be had.

TAs require a clarity regarding their role in lessons.

TAs require training and preparation.

How can the DR GOPTA and MR CHUFFI agendas support TAs in their work?

If TAs are to support teachers in differentiating appropriately and including pupils with SpLDs, there has to be a shared understanding of the purpose and strategy for support. The aspects of teaching and learning spelled out by MR CHUFFI can offer the TA a rationale for support, and the opportunities for access spelled out by DR GOPTA can highlight opportunities to diversify and support the approach.

For teachers working with support staff, there's a fine line between meeting their responsibility to pupils with identified learning needs and providing training. One of the reasons that so many of the ineffective practices cited earlier persist would appear to be the lack of a clear and consistent structure identifying who is responsible for making sure the TA/teacher relationship works. Negotiating the spaces in this relationship created by ambiguity and assumptions, coupled with gaps in understanding, can become an unhelpful drain on resources and morale.

With a view to closing those gaps and creating clarity of purpose, the following tools can be used to support the teacher-led approaches to differentiation by ensuring the TAs are clear about both the outcomes sought and the strategies to be employed in terms of any aspect of the opportunities for access to successful teaching and learning outlined in Chapter 6.

Familiarity with the DR GOPTA and MR CHUFFI agendas can provide a framework for effective pupil support enabling teacher/TA collaboration.

Self-evaluation and reference to the DR GOPTA framework can support teachers in directing differentiation.

Dialogue

One of the key findings of the DISS was that TAs often shut down the learning process for pupils with whom they worked by using closed questions and by retaining a focus on task completion.

The following tool can help teachers to be proactive and take the lead on learning in their own classrooms, while providing professional support for the support staff deployed into lessons.

The Teacher Talk Tally is a tool for TAs to use about teacher talk (Table 7.1). It provides an opportunity to focus on approaches to questioning, using the teacher's skills as a model. By focusing on teacher talk, it's possible to open a discussion about learning conversations and to promote the MR CHUFFI agenda, while at the same time gathering information about teaching habits and the impact of those habits on identified pupils.

The Classroom Talk Audit and contents of the Dialogue section in Chapter 6 can also be used by TAs to inform their work to support pupils.

Table 7.1 Teacher talk tally

Number of open questions	
Number of closed questions	
Number of instructions	
Phrases for praise	
Number of students praised	
Phrases for sanction	
Number of students sanctioned	
Phrases for checking understanding	
Phrases for dealing with the unexpected	
Minutes of silence	
Minutes of pupil talk/voice	

To what extent is my speech grammatically correct?	
Where do I speak from?	
Number of deliberate repetitions	
Number of requested repetitions	
Number of times I raise voice for attention	
Variation of tone and register	
Clarity of speech	
Pace of speech	

Resources

TAs can provide invaluable support to both teachers and to pupils with SpLDs simply by becoming aware of the variety of resources on offer to promote and facilitate the learning objectives.

Useful roles for TA regarding resources can be as facilitator, moderator or producer. However, this requires time and thought on the part of the teacher, who would need to offer the TA time to investigate and compile the necessary material, equipment or tools.

Table 7.2 Visual Cues Audit

MR CHUFFI	
Effective teaching	**Visual Cue**
Making Links	Themed table featuring labelled items with curricular relevance
Risk Taking	Lucky dip challenge box
Cognitive Engagement	Quote of the week as a prompt to ongoing discussion

(Continued)

Table 7.2 (Continued)

MR CHUFFI	
Effective teaching	**Visual Cue**
Higher Level Thinking	Question of the week wall – children can post a question to test their teacher.
Checking Understanding	Interactive diagrams to illustrate key facts, games to check understanding
Frequent Feedback	Simple criteria and tools to aid self-assessment
Fostering **I**ndependence	Personal project feature display

The Visual Cues Audit in Table 7.2 can offer a simple but effective framework to focus thinking about the use of visual cues to enable the pupil via the MR CHUFFI agenda. It can help TAs to identify relevant opportunities to use the resources already available and assist them to identify any additional resources that might be usefully created or purchased. The TA can also provide the teacher with helpful timely feedback in terms of which resources pupil find most attractive and usable ensuring that impact is at the centre of this aspect of provision.

TAs can support and maintain the production and use of Low-Tech Toolkits and the self-help strategies that accompany their use. Research has been scathing about the indiscriminate use of the highlighter pen as a learning enhancer, dismissing this activity as of little use in fixing knowledge and understanding to long-term memory (Coe, et al., 2014). Indiscriminate use is not advocated here; the Low-Tech Toolkit is designed to be used to reflect, revisit and signpost key information so that it may be located, used and considered in learning activities. It would be as easy to dismiss revision if revision was interpreted as literally seeing something again. The highlighters, sticky notes, coloured tabs, stickers and timers etc. that make up the kit can be used to support a struggling working memory in the same way a list helps the shopper to remember the ingredients of the cake; it does not replace the processes and reasoning that is required to engage with learning.

Grouping

The concerns raised by the DISS (Blatchford, et al., 2008) and the recommendations of the MITA (Sharples, et al., 2015) illustrate that isolation of pupils with SEN is often the result of the provision of one-to-one support from an adult in the classroom. This isolation from the social experience of learning comes in many forms, from a TA permanently seated next to a pupil acting as a filter for their participation in the lesson to a child spending considerable periods of time outside the classroom.

Placing TAs in a position where they can facilitate an approach to grouping which allows the pupil with Special Educational Needs Disability (SEND) to access the random, pupil- and teacher-chosen groups requires the clarity of communication preciously discussed.

Characteristics of best practice from TAs are not limited to specific SEN knowledge regarding targets, interventions, strategies and subject knowledge but extend to an agreement about how TAs should locate themselves in the classroom. Consideration of whether a TA is expected to sit or stand, for how long they should remain with one pupil and whether they need to sit next to a pupil to work with them is an important part of the plan. The simple questioning of the validity of a default setting about physical space can open a pupil's relationship to their peers and the classroom teacher.

Outcome

If the content of the learning can be addressed and achieved via a number of activities, all producing different outcomes, the TA has a valuable role in managing the plurality of classroom activities. For example, if the aim of the lesson is to understand the differences in plant and animal cells it's entirely possible that a pupil can show their knowledge and understanding via different media – in writing, in a diagram, a model etc. Simply by providing logistical support to the teacher an alternate way in to the learning can be offered and an outcome can be personalised.

Pace

The Pace section of Chapter 6 suggests four ways to consider pace: pace of speech; pace of processing; pace of the curriculum and time for repetition. The work of TAs is relevant in these respects. The Dialogue section of this chapter is likely to be of use to TAs when considering their approach to oracy and talk as a supportive strategy.

TAs have a vital role in highlighting issues of pace of learning that might arise for pupils with SpLDs. As TAs often experience material for the first time in lessons, alongside pupils, they are in a unique and valuable position to be objective in offering feedback to the teacher on the impact of their pace of delivery. The TA can highlight issues of pace or intervene on the part of pupils to ensure that they have sufficient processing time to consider material and to think. Pace of curriculum is most directly addressed by TAs in that often the evidence-based interventions run by TAs are skills related and allow the skills aspect of the curriculum to run at its own differentiated pace. Most essentially a TA can assist a pupil in returning to knowledge or concepts previously covered, facilitating the overlearning required to consolidate knowledge over time.

Task

The issues of differentiating by task outlined in this chapter point to TAs having a role in supporting the agenda for successful differentiation by task. It may be that the TA has non-contact time to assist the teacher in creating specific and personalised tasks for learning that build on strengths and existing progress. In the classroom the TA can promote the choices made by the pupil with SpLDs to undertake those tasks that underpin the activities promoted by the MR CHUFFI agenda. The TA can encourage the pupil to recognise their ability to take risks and learn from mistakes, building self-awareness and resilience rather than self-consciousness and dependency.

Assessment

Unless very carefully managed, assigning a role for the TA in this respect is potentially problematic. Providing feedback about the quality of a pupil's class work and homework is generally the province of the teacher. A TA may well be able to assist a pupil in understanding and using the feedback from a teacher or in interpreting the results of an assessment to inform their work. However, situations where a pupil might receive judgements about quality, effort or accuracy about the same piece of work from more than one source are to be avoided. At best it is duplication and at worst can cause confusion and lead to distress.

How can TAs work to support the MR CHUFFI agenda?

Moving away from a task-completion approach can be informed by familiarity with the aspects of effective teaching and learning promoted by the Mr CHUFFI and encourage TAs to look for opportunities for pupils with SpLDs to learn by Making Links, Taking Risks, Cognitively engaging, engaging in Higher level thinking, Checking Understanding, enabling meaningful Frequent Feedback and by Fostering Independence.

How can TAs foster independence?

There is something counter-intuitive about the notion of additional one-to-one support as a measure which can lead to greater independence. The research discussed earlier had much to say about increasing dependency as by-product of TA support. However, independence can be fostered by actively attending to the balance between the TA as a support mechanism and the TA as coach; the former mode provides access to the learning experience making it less risky, the latter mode as an agent of challenge, encouraging pupils to identify their own needs and to become more self-aware and self-reliant.

Is there a role for the TA in identification and monitoring?

The Needs Matrix featured in Chapter 3 offers an adaptable tool which can be used to focus the discussion around a pupil and target specific difficulties, needs, support, progress and attainment. By using a Needs Matrix or an adapted needs analysis the TA can be invited to offer regular, personalised feedback against a framework of informed and agreed priorities. This kind of objective and focused information can offer the teacher a broader context for consideration of the data gleaned from marking and assessments and help to plan classroom activities.

This approach and use of the Needs Matrix can be helpful in a single subject or across the curriculum. Clearly TAs are in a position to support a teaching and learning agenda set by the teacher within a particular year group, subject or discipline. However, TAs can also offer insight about the pupil across the curricular experience and their approach to learning in different situations including trips, clubs and recreation time. This essential role across more than one classroom and environment often places the TA in the position of expert when it comes to making a review of pupil progress. The Needs Matrix can be used by the TA to collect focused information across this range of experiences, informing the discussions about progress to include and develop the agenda set by pupil needs and shifting the balance of responsibility from the TA back to the teaching staff, having identified examples of the pupil's developing skills, strengths and weaknesses as they appear in context.

A tool for self-reflection

Classroom teachers are often in the slightly odd position of having a role in directing TAs but not in defining their role school-wide or line managing them. Ensuring that a shared understanding exists in terms of how the job specification translates into the classroom setting can be a useful and time-saving process.

The tool for self-reflection in Table 7.3 can be amended and used in training to discuss practice and to promote a practical set of guidelines for working with pupils in the classroom.

Table 7.3 In-class support practices

	In-class support practices	Never	Sometimes	Mostly	Always
1	I circulate in class rather than sit with identified pupils.				
2	Pupils know how to get my attention.				
3	I create visual aids/reminders in advance.				
4	I create visual aids and reminders in the classroom as required.				
5	I have a consistent support strategy which removes or reduces barriers to learning.				
6	I highlight and emphasise key points.				
7	I check before I chastise.				
8	I encourage risk-taking in learning.				
9	I enable teacher engagement/involvement with my target pupils.				
10	I record and share information about learning.				
11	I chunk tasks.				
12	I read for pupils.				
13	I scribe for pupils.				
14	I rephrase and re-explain tasks to pupils.				

(Continued)

Table 7.3 (Continued)

	In-class support practices	Never	Sometimes	Mostly	Always
15	I assist with behaviour management for all pupils.				
16	I use agreed strategies to manage the behaviour of target pupils.				
17	I have a toolkit for supporting memory.				
18	I have a sensory toolkit for supporting pupils with DCD and SID.				

Self-evaluation

What were the key messages from this chapter?

What do I need to review?

Which activities have I tried?

Which activities would I like to try?

Things I'd like to know more about:

Is this chapter relevant to a specific situation, pupil or class?

Chapter 8

How do I share good practice?

This penultimate chapter offers practical suggestions for using the tools in the book to assist in identifying and sharing good practice.

The chapter identifies the need for ongoing training about Special Educational Needs Disability (SEND) and the potential to use the training activities included in the book as part of regular practice and in support of an approach to Continued Professional Development that is sustained over time.

It goes on to look at ways to create, sustain and to develop a whole-school discourse about inclusive and effective teaching and learning for pupils with SEND.

It considers the value of working collaboratively to create a consistent approach to differentiated teaching that builds on existing skills and knowledge, identified by the opportunities for self-evaluation outlined in the book.

The chapter offers those in Leadership roles ideas for monitoring the impact of in-class provision and stresses the importance of including the views of children and families.

What is the role of the SENCO in supporting training and sharing good practice?

Special Educational Needs (SEN) provision is generally led by a SENCO or an Inclusion Manager. In this way SENCOs occupy a unique position in the senior management team. This flows from the fact that their job description, set out in the Special Educational Needs and Disability Code of Practice: 0–25 years, identifies a clear set of responsibilities not only in terms of this supervisory role but also in the training of, and development of competency in, their teaching colleagues. This is most apparent in terms of how the 'graduated approach' is implemented; 'The SENCO provides professional guidance to colleagues and will work closely with staff, parents and other agencies' (DFE, 2015, p. 108).

The strategic management and monitoring of SEND provision inevitably intersects with several key areas of whole-school responsibility, for unlike the leadership of a subject area, where there is a degree of distinct and discrete expertise and authority, the SENCO oversees a whole-school provision. If the school appoints an Inclusion Manager (who may be or may manage the SENCO) the role usually encompasses an additional degree of responsibility for the provision and performance of vulnerable and disadvantaged pupils at risk of underachievement and exclusion. These responsibilities may include safeguarding, equality of opportunity, pupil premium, EAL etc. However, it is the SENCO, not the Inclusion Manager, who is required to be named in the SEN Information Report (published on the school website) and who must undertake the National Award for Special Educational Needs Co-ordination within three years of appointment.

The SENCO also often manages a team of teaching staff, TAs and possibly specialists providing direct support and targeted 'interventions' across the whole school, in a variety of settings both curricular and extra curricular. In smaller schools the SENCO role is often subsumed into the role of an Assistant Head or a Deputy Head who works to lead and co-ordinate provision across the teaching staff in liaison with the various external agencies.

In characterising the role as one of co-ordinating provision, the implication is that the existing components of the provision are in place and it is for the SENCO simply to bring them together. Considering the range of SEN experience and gaps in SEN knowledge represented in any staff group, it's necessary to recognise the weight of responsibility this places on the SENCO, often the only member of a school team with an additional related qualification.

According to Her Majesty's Inspector, Lesley Cox, the National Lead for Special Educational Needs and Disability, 'Best practice is the result of good day to day training, supporting and management of teachers.' Unfortunately, there is not a one-off training experience that offers 'everything teachers need to know about SEND' that bridges the gaps and immediately lightens the workload of the teaching staff or the SENCO. Learning how to become a better practitioner in this respect is an ongoing, iterative, process – which is not helped by the tendency to use training time to brief teachers on what they are expected to deliver in the classroom, rather than to equip them to do it. To achieve the kind of deep learning that truly develops practice, it's necessary to move beyond the one-stop-shop, twilight training model and to look at how we can optimise and build upon the existing skill, specialism and motivation that exists within every school setting.

The 2004 the study entitled 'Teaching Strategies and Approaches for Pupils with Special Educational Needs' (Florian & Davis, 2004) identified that the problem is not the availability of effective strategies but how to create the conditions in which these strategies can be appropriately applied. It offered an insight into the tension that exists in attempting to implement theoretical research in everyday teaching practice. In my experience ineffective models of training often promote new solutions to teachers in the same, indiscriminate manner, we might apply a software patch to an IT problem.

Teacher training has real shortcomings in preparing teachers to meet the expectations regarding SEND.

The SENCO can provide essential support and guidance in making provision for pupils with SEND.

The SENCO is usually but not always a member of the Senior Leadership Team.

For training to influence practice it must take account of context and build on rather than replace skills and knowledge.

How do I identify teaching that 'works' for pupils with SpLD?

The success or failure of teachers in making appropriate in-class provision for pupils with learning difficulties has proved extremely difficult to analyse, to track and indeed to replicate. Ofsted are explicit in that 'Inspectors must not advocate a particular method of planning, teaching or assessment' (Ofsted, 2017b, p. 11). The 2004 study managed to identify 'promising approaches' to teaching pupils with SEN but identified a lack of evidence from research which might explain and characterise the success of some expert teachers in their ability 'to embed a responsiveness to individual need within the context of whole class teaching' (Florian & Davis, 2004, p. 36).

Best practice in relation to all aspects of education, from inclusive teaching to leadership, is defined in relation to pupil outcomes; thus progress and attainment measures, attendance and other forms of qualitative data and summative assessment are the gold standard for making judgements. However, it is very difficult to ascribe the pupil's success or failure to a specific provision, a mode of differentiation or an alternative approach unless the focus is narrow and specific. The pupil outcome may be the result of a complex interconnected provision made by more than one professional in more than one setting, making it extremely difficult to ascertain the worth differentiated teaching and to identify the most effective means of in-class support for pupils with SpLD.

Three straightforward ways to obtain feedback about teaching are to study the work product produced, to observe pupils working and to ask.

Finding ways to record, recall and share information about what has worked is an essential part of effective inclusive practice and refers back to a school's need to continue to 'build upon the pattern of learning and experience already established'. Schools expend huge resources in bringing professionals together to meet and to share information about teaching and learning in relation to pupils SpLD that is largely chronological in structure and subjective in nature. Setting an agenda for outcomes is one important aspect of the process of meeting needs, but developing a strategy across the curriculum and a toolbox of effective teaching practices is equally important.

All teachers are important to SEND provision and as such should be involved in sharing feedback.

Effective SEND provision has an identifiable rational, is consistent and benefits pupils.

Using a simple table to record participation in the MR CHUFFI agenda (see Table 8.1) provides a teacher with useful information about how pupils respond to differentiated teaching. This information can be collected and collated simply and quickly in a wide variety of ways either following or during teaching via:

- a book look;
- marking; and
- a discussion with a pupil led by a TA or Teacher.

It's possible to use this framework to focus on the learning habits of a specific individual, to compare individuals or cohorts in a class; to work with a colleague to compare feedback in different subjects and settings, across curricula on a single day; to track behaviour in a specific subject, to consider different strategies for differentiation; or to inform a focused observation by a colleague.

The chart can be collated with specific pupil names and comments about their work and learning behaviour or as a tally chart that enables a teacher to compare the engagement of different groups of pupils.

Table 8.1 Compare SEND and non-SEND pupils

MR CHUFFI agenda	SEND pupils	Non-SEND pupils	Comment or support
			DR GOPTA
Making Links	JH, TM, LV		Worked with peer group to discuss and present views – LSA provided visual cue and prompt for time
Risk Taking	NJ		
Cognitive Engagement	MN KS MN		
Checking Understanding			
Higher Level thinking			
Frequent **F**eedback			
Fostering **I**ndependence			

In using the MR CHUFFI and DR GOPTA frameworks for targeting support, it is possible to record and consider information about successful approaches to teaching and learning in the light of pupil outcomes. In addition, it's possible to collect feedback about pupil engagement in learning activities. This enables the teacher, the TA and the SENCO to see the evidence of any correlation between your efforts to adapt and differentiate teaching and higher levels of achievement.

By shifting the focus from SEN discussions around whether or not a pupil has met an individual target to encompass instead how a pupil met the target through their learning behaviour, level of participation and engagement, it's possible for teachers to obtain and to share an overview of pupil engagement across the curriculum and as such inform their approach to differentiation and more inclusive practice. Instead of simply celebrating the product of learning it is vital that the process of learning that has proved successful receives similar attention. Essentially, the model for sharing good practice promoted here has, at its heart, the ownership of the rationale underpinning the practice and against which the outcomes can be considered. Sharing experiences about teaching SpLD pupils with colleagues based on a common purpose, understanding, language and format helps teachers to focus on improving practice rather than creating series of narratives.

What forums exist for sharing good practice about SEND?

The nature and frequency of the points of contact necessary to facilitate and reflect on a school's in-class SEN provision vary. Most frequently, they coalesce around the progress and performance of individual pupils. Teachers are regularly asked to participate in the discussion around identified pupils and to provide feedback on progress, offer samples of work and occasionally submit their planning at times of review, consultation, inspection or transition. The focus for the individual teacher is usually on how a pupil is responding to teaching and progressing in the context of the specific demands of the curriculum.

Other opportunities for a focus on SEN might include:

Learning walks: From time to time personalised provision and differentiation may be the focus of learning walls and observation at which time teachers are likely to have the opportunity to discuss this aspect of their planning and delivery with senior colleagues and possibly the SENCO.

Departmental meetings: In some larger settings there may be a designated member of a subject team who works with the SENCO to coordinate delivery of the SEN provision. Where this model is used there may be a regular opportunity to talk through issues, receive training and share good practice at a departmental level.

Working in collaboration: One of the most frequent points of contact with the school SEN provision is in working collaboratively with TAs in the classroom. It may be that communication with TAs forms the primary point of contact with the SENCO and external agencies. Collaboration may take place in the form of taking part in the work of the Support Department, via involvement in the delivery of a specific programme of intervention or as a result of some additional specialist training.

School improvement: When the school is involved with a school improvement service or partner or conducting a review of SEND provision there may be times for focused discussion of classroom practice focused on differentiation and other inclusive practice.

Special interest groups: It's not uncommon for schools to run parent and staff special interest groups around SEN to share knowledge, specialism and practice.

It's therefore necessary to create systems that encourage teachers to reflect on their classroom practice regarding all aspects of the graduated approach from initial identification to making and reviewing provision for identified pupils.

The audit tools and activities in this book offer an adaptable set of templates for recording and sharing the processes of preparation, planning, teaching and feedback that underpin the provision of an effective graduated approach.

What systems exist for pupils and families of pupils with EHC plans and those on SEN support to offer feedback in regard to classroom teaching?

It may be that an Annual Review–type system of meetings operates not only for pupils with Education, Health and Care (EHC) plans but also those on SEN support. Generally, preparation for Annual Reviews involves a consultative process where the views of children and their families are sought in advance. In the context of an Annual Review the feedback should allow a Local Education Authority to make an explicit link between the way a school is going about making provision and the impact of the that provision on a pupil's progress and attainment. However due to the highly pressured nature of the meetings – where often a single child is in discussing the learning in a room literally full of adults – the pupil's comments are monosyllabic and of little real help in identifying the strengths and weaknesses of provision from the pupil's perspective.

While it is highly desirable to make space for the voice of a pupil and their family in Annual Review it is very difficult to unpick the role of differentiated class teaching in the success of a special provision made via EHC plan or within the school's resources.

Taking steps to gather feedback pupil in the course of teaching is a valuable way of ensuring pupil voice that speaks directly and accurately to the quality and the nature of in class provision. Pupils are often asked to comment on the aspects of provision they find most helpful after the fact rather than being invited to consider and comment on the way they are supported in context.

The quality of pupil feedback can vary enormously depending on the approach taken to the conversation and the questions asked.

When seeking pupil feedback about provision:

- review skills for good listening in Chapter 6;
- agree upon a process with the pupil first (during or after the lesson, in class or on one-to-one time);
- share the purpose of the conversation;
- don't insist on participation;
- actively welcome all contributions – all feedback is good feedback;
- seek feedback from non-SEND pupils as a control;
- include open questions;
- focus some questions on any aspect of the strategy employed.
- have materials to hand that might act as a reminder for the lesson; and
- thank the pupil for sharing their views.

How can I continue to develop the skills and knowledge needed to support pupils with SEND?

Teachers tend to have an idiosyncratic journey through Continual Professional Development and it's hard to see how the training offer matches up to the expectations implicit in the law and the regulations.

In January 2015 the Carter Review of Initial Teacher Training (ITT) clarified a widely felt concern that teacher training had left graduates in a vulnerable position, in terms of their preparedness to teach pupils with learning difficulties and associated Special Educational Needs (SEN). ITT programmes were found to be inconsistent and to offer very restricted time to address the issues:

> Throughout this review, organisations have raised concerns with us about how ITT inadequately prepares new teachers to address special educational needs and disabilities. We acknowledge that it can be challenging to address SEND within Initial Teacher Training programmes, particularly those that are one-year long. However, we feel there is too much variability across the system in what is covered in SEND.
>
> (Carter, 2015, p. 11, v)

As a result, SEND has now found its place as an obligatory part of all ITT Programmes. The Swiss Cottage/IOE study 'Towards a New Reality for Teacher Education for SEND'[1] published in March 2015 moved the conversation on with a detailed report of more than 100 pages. The study strongly recommended more training time for SEND and also recognised the significant restrictions on time exerted by a 10-month ITT course, the majority of which is spent in placement.

Despite concerns about ITT, Continual Professional Development (or in-service training) can offer an ongoing opportunity to enhance knowledge and skills. Unfortunately, this much-needed training offer is often limited and irregular as there is no legal duty on schools to provide regular SEND training in the same way there is to provide professional training on Child Protection and Safeguarding.

The research on the subject supports the message from teachers, parents and SEN charities that more ongoing training and support is necessary for both newly qualified and experienced teachers.

The good news is that some training opportunities will be made available via whole-staff training at your school. Try to ensure attendance at upcoming training events. There are also often low cost, local, day or short courses offered by external providers or the Local Authority. It may be that the school SENCO has a surgery or drop-in sessions or takes part in an induction programme. If the school is providing training to TAs or groups of staff on a voluntary basis, be sure to invest in your own learning and try to attend. Performance Management should include a discussion of training requirements – and showing interest in learning is never a bad thing, so do ask about opportunities.

Courses are delivered by wide range of providers including universities, private consultants, Local Authorities and charities. For those wishing to learn in greater depth or to specialise in teaching pupils with SpLD, there is usually a decision to make in terms of choosing between specialist teaching and therapeutic practice or SEND educational management. The charities most active in providing training tend to focus on specific areas of need and provide focused courses for parents, individuals and educators. The Bibliography at the back of this book contains a list of links to the training pages of a number of UK SEND charities.

Social media have provided an invaluable source of insight and inspiration for me as a school leader and as a consultant, allowing me to connect with practitioners, academics, charities, families and pressure groups and discover a wider discourse both in the UK and overseas. Looking beyond the teaching blogs and conventional commentators to the work undertaken by pressure groups and charities has added immeasurably to my understanding of this highly complex and diverse aspect of education.

The DR GOPTA and MR CHUFFI agendas can provide a common language and a flexible framework for feedback about SEND provision.

It's important to consider opportunities for pupil feedback.

Its helpful to have a broad view of training and to be aware of the variety of both educational and specialist providers and platforms.

Two heads are better than one – collaborate.

Self-evaluation

What were the key messages from this chapter?

What do I need to review?

Which activities have I tried?

Which activities would I like to try?

Things I'd like to know more about?

Is this chapter relevant to a specific situation, pupil or class?

Note

1 Joseph Mintz, Margaret Mulholland, Nick Peacey UCL Institute of Education and Swiss Cottage School Development and Research Centre, *Towards a New Reality for Teacher Education for SEND*, www.ucl.ac.uk/ioe/departments-centres/centres/centre-for-inclusive-education/send-in-initial-teacher-training-project/pdfs/send-in-itt-roadmap-summary

Chapter 9

How do I implement change?

This short chapter invites the reader to record and reflect on the tasks they have completed throughout the book. In doing so the book itself is offered as a tool for the planning and implementation of new approaches to differentiating teaching. It outlines the importance of creating useful habits and outlines a process for self-evaluation, looking at the benefits of collaborative working and a 'less is more' approach.

In-service training time is often used to introduce changes to working practices. Continual Professional Development schedules can become populated with briefings concerned with the imposition of changes driven and directed by external or even circumstantial factors. This can result in a somewhat awkward and defensive attitude towards training, especially if it fails to create the essential links between the big-picture and the day-to-day experience of the workforce.

When training is pedagogical and research-based it can prove similarly uncomfortable. While educational research can do much to invigorate the ongoing discourse about effective teaching, this often comes in the form of a school's pursuit or promotion of a single, ideal pedagogical model. Over time teachers experience a layering of one set of educational principles and practices upon another. This approach to training leaves teachers little time for consideration of the specific circumstances, the assimilation of facts and the adaptation of existing practice that leads to the development of good on-the-spot judgement.

How do I implement change in the classroom?

When I deliver training about Special Educational Needs (SEN) to groups of teachers I'm often asked to make it practical and easy to implement. School leaders want me to focus on teaching strategies, techniques and materials that 'work' with pupils who are struggling: a new strategy to support reading, a new programme to help pupils to plan their essays, the best book to use when developing vocabulary or social communication. In such a context a change in practice is characterised as something that happens immediately and manifests externally, as new language, materials and equipment all of which can be used by teachers in the classroom.

Whilst it's likely that some of this may be part of implementing a change that sees a struggling pupil flourish, the actions taken to differentiate are always going to require consideration of the context. There is no one-size-fits-all when it comes to making provision for pupils with SpLD.

Its undoubtedly useful to have immediate access to an array of tools, resources and strategies; however, without a rationale for their use their impact is likely to be limited. More importance has to be placed on the impact of a change in attitude that can come from a greater understanding of learning difficulties, SpLDs and Special Educational Needs Disability (SEND). The way we think and the ways we structure our thinking regarding making appropriate provision for pupils with SEN is arguably more important, and considerably more lasting, than the materials and techniques we employ. Without acknowledging that our teaching practice relates to a set of beliefs about our pupils, it's unlikely that changes will be consistent and of benefit to them.

For this reason, the training activities included in this book invite teachers to consider models of good practice for differentiation, via a process of self-evaluation. By thinking through their existing practices, attitudes and beliefs about their current pupils teachers may come to understand the changes which are possible.

How do I create useful habits?

Making changes to established habits appears to be just about the hardest thing for an adult to do. Harm, peril, misery or futility are often not strong enough factors in themselves to counter habitual behaviour. It takes us time to assimilate messages about the meaning and impact of our habits and even longer to act to change them. Change requires the fulfilment of the following conditions:

Appetite: In order to make any kind of change and do it successfully you have to want something that you don't currently have access to – whether it's money, a good night's sleep, a happier pupil, a higher reading age or a faster time over 5K. The goal of the change must be tangible and clear. Taking action to develop knowledge and skills in regard to effective differentiation might be in response to a course of study or in response to some specific problems you're experiencing in the classroom. Despite the fact that, in order to make progress, it might be necessary to begin with a description of the problem, it's also necessary to imagine and to describe what the resolution might look like and for whom.

Effort: It takes time and effort to establish a change and for the change to become a habit. Developing new skills requires practice. Don't expect to be an instant expert or go for the satisfying quick fix. When something is difficult or unfamiliar it can feel like it takes longer than it does. It can be helpful to be clear about how many times and for how long have you tried a new approach or strategy with a pupil before making a judgement or collating the feedback about its impact.

Courage: Change can be disorientating. Using new technology, changing groupings or classroom environment can feel like an exposing and somewhat thankless task, especially if the rewards are not immediately apparent. Processes of self-evaluation put the automatic, unconscious and routine back into the visible realm of planned action. Recognise the difficulty and acknowledge the difference between the way you feel about it and what you think about it.

Acceptance of failure: Inevitably you will fail some of the time. Don't be alarmed by it; expect it. Our biggest and most painful failures are often our most important learning experiences. Teachers are human – not superheroes. Experimentation requires acceptance of feedback, good and bad. One of my worst mistakes as a new SENCO was a simple inability to delegate properly. I asked a member of my team to prepare a letter for parents, and did so without specifying my expectations. Following her completion of the task I was critical of her work: it simply wasn't done in the way I had expected, and I re-drafted the letter. Thankfully she was assertive enough to speak to me about it and we had a frank but professional conversation about how my actions had affected her, wasting her time and effort by failing to be clear about what I wanted. I learned so much from that embarrassing mistake: not to make assumptions, to be clear about expectations, to be respectful of people's time, to be more considerate of the feelings of team members and not to lose sight of the bigger picture in pursuit of powering through tasks.

Honesty: Face the facts and be honest with peers and with yourself. Embracing the feedback involves ascribing the same value to praise as to criticism. Understanding the value of criticism, even if it simply reveals misunderstanding or scarcity of facts, is essential to progress. If the goals for the change have been clearly established it's possible to determine whether they have been reached.

Self-Evaluation: Give yourself some love for the work you are doing, actively, regularly and in whatever form that nurture comes. Take time, whether it's with family, yourself, your dog, your paints, your bike or your books. Be appreciative of yourself and your contribution. There will always be more work than can be fitted into hours in the day and so making time for rest and a little self-appreciation is an absolute necessity.

In making a change, use Table 9.1 to identify and record

Table 9.1 Implementing change

What do I want?	**Appetite**
What am I doing?	**Effort**
How does it feel?	**Courage**
What went wrong?	**Obstacles**
What feedback is there?	**Honesty**
What am I doing to support myself?	**Nurture**

How do I identify and adopt good habits for differentiated teaching?

It could be argued that implementing change is a teacher's core business. By its nature, teaching and learning exists to facilitate changes in understanding and opportunity. In addition, the cyclical way in which teaching and learning is organised in schools presents teachers with new faces each September and along with it new curricula, new systems and new pedagogies.

Teachers must manage this constant tide of change while projecting levels of confidence and competence consistent with a role that embodies stability, reliability and consistency. It requires huge skill and stamina to balance the changing intellectual and emotional demands of such a role within the tight constraints of the environment, the timetable and exacting performance standards.

Considering these demands and constraints, a degree of automaticity is a basic requirement for survival. Routine creates boundaries, stability and ease; it exists to make the unpredictable, predictable. An established modus operandi automatically reduces, edits or even eliminates the tsunami of choice, opportunity and distraction produced in the daily life of the classroom, transforming it into a more manageable pyramid of priorities.

We create routines for our working life in the same way as we create them for every other aspect of our behaviour. We have preferred routines for the way we eat, the way we dress, the way we travel to work in the same way as we have a routine way of organizing our desk, diaries and resources. As these routines become established they become habitual, requiring less conscious thought and action.

If teachers are to give due consideration to the special educational needs of their pupils it's necessary that two of the habits they develop are self-awareness and adaptability. These two features of practice help us to avoid a situation in which the way we do our work is the result of a thousand little, unconscious, decisions made while we were hard at work solving something bigger and more pressing.

The approach to training and Continual Professional Development taken in these pages is incremental; all of the audits and surveys require a degree of self-awareness. The psychology says that if we can first become aware of our habits and recognise the choice we made in adopting them, we can choose to modify them and to change them. To improve it's necessary to ask, 'Are we aware of our habits and are they good?'

To consolidate and enhance knowledge and skills, meaningful professional development requires the acknowledgement of existing practice and an appraisal of the knowledge and understanding on which that practice is based.

How can this book help me to develop self-awareness and adaptability in teaching pupils with SpLD?

The DR GOPTA and MR CHUFFI agendas detailed in Chapter 6 bring together and expand upon the suggested criteria for self-evaluation historically promoted by Ofsted. The mnemonics provide simple structures for thinking about inclusive teaching that can be kept in mind while preparing, planning, teaching and sharing feedback.

Ofsted have repeatedly invited teachers to consider that good structures for self-evaluation should include: subject knowledge; the role of teachers as learners; effective modelling; planning that has continuity building on skills and knowledge; the level of pupil engagement; appeal to higher level thinking; asking probing questions; provision for practical work for all abilities; and effective and frequent feedback.

The tools, checklists and audits in this book are designed to form a self-evaluative survey of existing attitudes and teaching habits in making provision for pupils with SpLDs and SEN, examining preferred approaches and any 'default settings'. The surveys provide a comprehensive set of suggestions for diversifying approaches to teaching and learning.

Using the tools and audits in the book to reflect on current practice can offer the reassurance that comes from identifying the existing rationale, consistency and benefit of the current approach, while providing an opportunity to identify gaps in knowledge and plan a way forward.

A change to practice should be the result of a development in thinking.

Making a change is involves appetite, effort, courage, failure, honesty and self-care.

Change is an active process and may require planning and preparation.

The book can be used as a record and a plan of action.

In creating an Action Plan for implementation of new strategies for differentiation either use the self-evaluation which appears at the end of each chapter to indicate which of the activities have already been completed, or use the book itself as a diary to record the work done so far:

1 Pick two colours of sticky tabs.
2 Use one to indicate an action taken, a change or an activity that you have tried.
3 Use a second colour to indicate something you might like to try in future.
4 For evaluation purposes, date the tab and indicate the initials of the pupil or the class you hope to impact.

The traditional to-do list always seems to eradicate our achievements by crossing them through while endlessly focusing attention on what's still left to do. Using coloured tabs in this way results in a more encouraging, time-related and comprehensive record of action taken to develop practice in regard to supporting pupils with SpLDs.

Have I improved my understanding of key terms and concepts?

Review the self-evaluations at the end of each chapter and consider concepts that remain unclear and require review.

Which of the activities have I tried?

Use the self-evaluation at the end of each chapter to record progress so far.
    Having considered your progress with the content so far it may be helpful to

1 Try completing Table 9.1.
2 Revisit a specific chapter and to complete more of the activities.
3 Review one or more of the concepts that are still unclear or refer to the sources or notes listed at the back of the book to gain clarification.
4 Find a study partner or group with whom you can collaborate and share workload.
5 Enlist the support of an LSA and TA to support feedback and to participate in the activities.
6 Look at your schedule and consider a realistic timeline for any of these actions.

Why is working collaboratively important?

The downside to educational consultancy is (for the most part) working alone. When you work surrounded by colleagues in a school it's easy to take for granted the joy of being part of a team, a group of people brought together by a shared purpose and a shared experience. Over and above trying the structured, practice-sharing, activities included in this book, it's important not to overlook the value of finding a collaborator with whom to discuss your work. A fruitful professional partnership can be forged outside of your Year Group, your subject or your specialism, and can shed light on your study style and your routines for preparation and teaching. You are surrounded by professional teachers; there is so much to learn from each other. Collaborate!
    Some of the little things I learned from colleagues that changed my working life and made it better:

- Only diarise in pencil – things change.
- Be explicit when delegating a task and allow colleagues to take responsibility.

- Never give exclusively negative feedback to anyone.
- Turn over alternate pages in notebooks and diaries, bottom corner to top corner, and vice versa, so that today miraculously appears.
- In training or teaching use lights or music, instead of voice, as a signal to request quiet.
- When you don't know what to say, or how to answer a question, wait and ask for time to think.
- Proof-read for spelling backwards from the end of a text to the beginning.
- Avoid fluorescent lighting at all costs.
- Don't look at email before going to sleep (staying awake).
- Practice yoga.
- Never re-read yesterday's pages before starting today's (without this advice I'd still be on page 1).

Self-evaluation

What were the key messages from this chapter?

What do I need to review?

Which activities have I tried?

Which activities would I like to try?

Things I'd like to know more about?

Is this chapter relevant to a specific situation, pupil or class?

Bibliography

Books and articles

Alexander-Passe, N., 2015. *Dyslexia and Mental Health*. London: Jessica Kingsley.

Alloway, R. & Alloway, T., 2013. *The Working Memory Advantage*. New York: Simon and Schuster.

Barrow, H., Clark, A. & Hartley, K., 2012. Unmet Need in Scotland's Criminal Justice System, *Bulletin of Royal College of Speech and Language Therapists*. February 2012, pp. 20–21.

Bartlett, J., 2016. *Outstanding Differentiation for Classroom Learning*. First ed. London and New York: David Fulton/Routledge.

Bergquist, W. H. & Phillips, S. R., 1977. *A Handbook for Faculty Development*, Volume 2. Washington, DC: Council for the Advancement of Small Colleges.

Blatchford, P. et al., 2008. *The DISS Project*. London: Institute of Education, University of London.

Blum-Ross, A. & Livingstone, S., 2015. *Families and Screen Time: Current Advice and Emerging Research*. Media Policy Brief 17. London: The London School of Economics and Political Science.

Carter, S. A., 2015. *Carter Review of Initial Teacher Training*. s.l.: Crown.

Coe, R., Aloisi, C., Higgins, S. & Major, L. E., 2014. *What Makes Great Teaching: A Review of the Underpinning Research*. s.l.: Sutton Trust, Durham University, CEM.

Collins-Donnelly, K., 2012. *Starving the Anger Gremlin*. London: Jessica Kingsley.

Collins-Donnelly, K., 2014. *Banish Your Self-Esteem Thief*. London: Jessica Kingsley.

Davis, P. & Florian, L., 2004. *Teaching Strategies and Approaches for Pupils with Special Educational Needs: A Scoping Study*. London: University of Cambridge, University of Manchester, DFES.

DFE, 2011. *Teacher's Standards*. London: Department for Education.

DFE, 2015. *Keeping Children Safe in Education: Statutory Guidance for Schools and Colleges, March 2015*. London: Department for Education.

DFE, 2016a. *Children with Special Educational Needs and Disabilities (SEND)*. London: Department for Education.

DFE, 2016b. *School Workforce in England 2016*. s.l.: Department for Education.

DFE, 2017. *Statistical First Release 37/2017, Special Educational Needs in England*. London: Department for Education.

DFE, 2017–18. *School Census*. London: Department for Education.

DFE & DoH, 2015. *SEND Code of Practice 0–25 Years*. London: Department for Education, Department of Health.

Didau, D., 2016. *What If Everything You Knew about Teaching Was Wrong?* Wales: Crown House Publishing Company.

Driver Youth Trust, 2013. *The Fish in the Tree: Why We Are Failing Children with Dyslexia?* Driver Youth Trust. Available from http://cdn.basw.co.uk/upload/basw_15304-3.pdf

Dweck, C., 2017. *Mindset*. London, UK: Little, Brown Book Company.

Dyslexia Action, 2013. *Dyslexia and Literacy Difficulties: Policy and Practice Review, a Consensus Call for Action: Why, What and How?* The Dyslexia-SpLD Trust. Available from www.thedyslexia-spldtrust.org.uk

Eide, B. L. & Eide, F. F., 2011. *The Dyslexic Advantage*. London and New York: Hay House.

Elliot, V. et al., 2016. *A Marked Improvement? A Review of the Evidence of Written Marking*. London: EEF/University of Oxford.

Equality and Human Rights Commission, 2015. *Reasonable Adjustments for Disabled Pupils*. Equality and Human Rights Commission. Available from https://www.equalityhumanrights.com/en/publication-download/reasonable-adjustments-disabled-pupils

Florian, L. & Davis, P., 2004. *Teaching Strategies and Approaches for Pupils with Special Educational Needs: A Scoping Study*. s.l.: DFES.

Florian, L., Tilston, C. & Rose, R., 1998. *Inclusive Practice: What? Why? and How? Promoting Inclusive Practice*. London: Routledge.

Foss, B., 2013. *The Dyslexia Empowerment Plan*. New York: Ballantine Books.

Gershon, M., 2013. *How to Use Differentiation in the Classroom: The Complete Guide*. CreateSpace Independent Publishing Platform.

Hume, C. & Snowling, M. J., 2009. *Developmental Disorders of Language Learning and Cognition*. Oxford: Wiley-Blackwell.

Independent Teacher Workload Review Group, 2016. Eliminating unnecessary workload around marking. www.gov.uk/government/publications/reducing-teacher-workload-marking-policy-review-group-report

Ko, J., Sammons, P. & Bakkum, L., 2014. *Effective Teaching*. s.l.: Education Development Trust.

Office for Standards in Education, 2017a. *OfSTED Inspections: Myths*. London: OfSTED.

Office for Standards in Education, 2017b. *School Inspections Handbook*. London: OfSTED.

OECD, 2014. Indicator D1: How much time do students spend in the classroom?, in *Education at a Glance 2014: OECD Indicators*. Paris: OECD Publishing. http://dx.doi.org/10.1787/888933119530.

O'Hare, A., & Khalid, S. (2002). The association of abnormal cerebellar function in children with developmental coordination disorder and reading difficulties. *Dyslexia, 8*, 234–248.

Peer, L. & Reid, G., 2001. *Dyslexia: Successful Inclusion in the Secondary School*. London: David Fulton.

Rooke, M., 2016. *Creative Successful Dyslexic*. London: Jessica Kingsley.

Sharples, J., Webster, R. & Blatchford, P., 2015. *Making Best Use of Teaching Assistants Guidance Report*. London: Education Endowment Foundation.

Online references

BBC Active, Methods of Differentiation in the Classroom. www.bbcactive.com/BBCActiveIdeasandResources/MethodsofDifferentiationintheClassroom.aspx

Biel, Lindsey, and Nancy Peske, Sensory Smarts, Raising a Sensory Smart Child. www.sensorysmarts.com/working_with_schools.html

The British Dyslexia Association, What Are Specific Learning Difficulties? www.bdadyslexia.org.uk/educator/what-are-specific-learning-difficulties

Collins, Nick, IQ Tests 'Do Not Reflect Intelligence', *Daily Telegraph*, 2012. www.telegraph.co.uk/news/science/science-news/9755929/IQ-tests-do-not-reflect-intelligence.html

Counselling Directory, Risk Factors. www.counselling-directory.org.uk/young-people-stats.html#riskfactors

The Education Endowment Foundation, Learning Styles, Jan 2018. https://educationendowmentfoundation.org.uk/resources/teaching-learning-toolkit/learning-styles/

The Education Endowment Foundation, What Do Standardised Tests Offer That Teacher Assessment Can't? https://educationendowmentfoundation.org.uk/tools/assessing-and-monitoring-pupil-progress/testing/standardised-tests/

The e-learning Network, Ruby Rumson, 'Coffield et al – Critique of Learning Styles' June 2017. http://resources.eln.io/coffield-critique-of-learning-styles/

Frank, Liz, 5 Ways You Are Failing Students With Learning Difficulties, *Huffpost, The Blog*. www.huffingtonpost.com/liz-frank/5-ways-you-are-failing-students-with-learning-disabilities_b_6751890.html

Gardiner, Bonnie and Hannah Thompson, YouGov UK. https://yougov.co.uk/news/2012/04/27/holding-pupils-back-year/

Gov.uk. Schools' Financial Efficiency: Top 10 Planning Checks for Governors. www.gov.uk/guidance/schools-financial-efficiency-top-10-planning-checks-for-governors#staff-pay-as-percentage-of-total-expenditure

Jeffreys, Branwen (Ed.), Horrendous Meltdowns: Why I Home-Educate My Daughter, 27 November 2017. www.bbc.co.uk/news/education-42103248

McLeod, Saul, Working Memory, *Simply Psychology*, 2008. www.simplypsychology.org/working%20memory.html

Mintz, Joseph, Margaret Mulholland, and Nick Peacey, UCL Institute of Education and Swiss Cottage School Development and Research Centre. www.ucl.ac.uk/ioe/departments-centres/centres/centre-for-inclusive-education/send-in-initial-teacher-training-project/pdfs/send-in-itt-roadmap

Moll, Kristina, Dyslexia and Co-morbid Disorders, University of York, 2012. www.dyslexia.bangor.ac.uk/documents/KMollLectureNotes.pdf

Morin, Amanda, Understood, Multi-sensory Instruction. www.understood.org/en/school-learning/partnering-with-childs-school/instructional-strategies/multisensory-instruction-what-you-need-to-know

Optimus Education, What Do We Really Mean by Quality First Teaching? *Knowledge Centre*, March 2015. http://my.optimus-education.com/what-do-we-really-mean-quality-first-teaching

Royal College of Speech and Language Therapists. 2018. Overview of Language Disorder. www.rcslt.org/clinical_resources/language_disorder/overview

The Royal College of Speech and Language Therapists, The Box, Speech and Language Therapy and the Criminal Justice Sector. www.theboxtraining.com/about-us/speech-and-language-therapy-and-criminal-justice-sector

Success.com, Personal Development, 2016. www.success.com/article/why-bad-habits-are-so-easy-to-make-and-so-hard-to-break

The International Dyslexia Association, Multisensory Structured Language Teaching. https://dyslexiaida.org/multisensory-structured-language-teaching/

Teacher Tools, Differentiation. http://teachertools.londongt.org/?page=differentiationClassRoom

Teaching for Neurodiversity: A Guide to Specific Learning Difficulties. www.bdadyslexia.org.uk/common/ckeditor/filemanager/userfiles/Delegates_pack_Primary/A_Guide_to_SpLD_Primary.pdf

Tirraoro, Tania, Special Educational Needs Finally to Be Part of England's Core Teacher Training, July 2016. www.specialneedsjungle.com/special-educational-needs-finally-england-core-teacher-training/

Links to regulations

The Children and Families Act, www.legislation.gov.uk/ukpga/2014/6/contents

Equality Act 2010, www.legislation.gov.uk/ukpga/2010/15/contents

The Special Educational Needs and Disability (Send) Regulations 2014, www.legislation.gov.uk/uksi/2014/1530/made

Links to organisations providing specialist advice and training on SpLD and SEND

The Driver Youth Trust http://driveryouthtrust.com

Dyslexia Action http://dyslexiaaction.org.uk/

Dyslexic Advantage http://dyslexicadvantage.org

The ADHD Foundation www.adhdfoundation.org.uk/

The National Autistic Society www.autism.org.uk/

The British Dyslexia Association www.bdadyslexia.org.uk/

Helen Arkell www.helenarkell.org.uk/

Independent Parental Special Education Advice www.ipsea.org.uk/

National Association of Special Educational Needs www.nasen.org.uk/

Academy of Orton-Gillingham Practitioners and Educatorswww.ortonacademy.org/approach.php

The Royal College of Speech and Language Therapists www.rcslt.org/about/introduction

Special Needs Jungle www.specialneedsjungle.com/

The Dyslexia SpLD Trust www.thedyslexia-spldtrust.org.uk/

Training experiences, seminars, schools, organisations, books and resources about SEND are showcased annually at two major SEN events

The TES SEN Show 2018
www.tessenshow.co.uk/

Resources

Here you will find blank copies of all training activities and checklists included throughout the book listed according to chapter. Photocopy and re-use as you wish.

Chapter 1: What do I know about Special Educational Needs Disability and inclusive teaching?

Table 1.1 Getting started

Getting started			
Questions	Yes	No	Information/action
Have I read the school SEND policy and or handbook?			
Have I read the school SEND Information report?			
Have I read the school's most recent inspection report or recent performance data?			
Am I aware of the nature of baseline information on *all* pupils in my class?			
Have I met the school SENCO?			
Have I visited any onsite SEND facilities?			
Am I clear about the process of referral?			
Am I clear about channels of communication with SEND staff?			

Chapter 2: What about a baseline?

Table 2.1 Collecting baseline data

Questions	Yes	No	Action/response
Is this group new to the school?			
Do I know what baseline data exist for this group?			
Do I have access to these baseline data?			
Have I looked at all of the baseline data for this group?			
Are any children missing from the information?			

Table 2.2 Looking at baseline data

Questions	Yes	No	Action/response
Are there any pupils whose individual scores vary widely?			
Are the pupils with very low reading scores?			
Are there any low attaining pupils with high baseline scores?			
Have I cross referenced the SEND data for identified students?			
Have I cross referenced data on gifted and talented pupils?			
Are there twice-exceptional pupils in the group?			
Is there a colleague who can support me in answering my questions?			
Can I access samples of the pupils' work?			

Table 2.3 Consulting specific baseline information about SEN support pupils

Questions	Yes	No	Action/response
Have I consulted the SEND register?			
Am I aware of the identified SEN support pupils in my class?			
Have I consulted their baseline data?			
Am I aware of any specific areas of strength or specific deficits?			
Have I read the available IEP or Pupil Passports?			
Have I accessed the supporting specialist reports?			

Table 2.4 Getting ready to teach pupils with EHC plans

Preparation	Yes	No	Information/action	Date
Name of pupil		**Haley Potter**		
Have I identified the pupils in my classes with EHC plans (or Statements)?				
Have I read the EHC plans Section B: describing learning difficulties and special educational needs?				
Have I read Section E describing outcome Section F describing provision?				
Are there any specific adjustments to be made to the environment to increase access?				
Am I aware of and competent to use any assistive technology (radio-mic etc.)?				
Do I know if there will be LSAs or Teaching Assistants (TAs) in any of my classes as a result of pupil SENDs?				
Will pupils be missing from my classes to attend interventions?				
Can I relate the specific outcomes identified on EHC plan directly to my teaching this term?				

Are there identifiable next steps towards EHC objectives for pupils this term?				
Have I agreed objectives with pupils?				
Have I introduced myself to and agreed a way to communicate with pupils?				
Have I seen samples of pupils' work in any subjects?				
Does an understanding exist about the role of the TAs or LSAs in supporting those objectives in my classroom?				
Have I agreed on a way to communicate with the TA or SEND team to review plans?				
Have I met the support staff with whom I will work?				
How, when and to whom do I feedback on progress?				
Dates of Annual Reviews?				
Dates of ongoing diagnostic assessments?				
Date of meeting with parents/family/pupil?				

Chapter 3: How do I identify learners with SEND? The Needs Matrix

Table 3.1 Needs Matrix

Current attainment in your subject	Rate behaviours affecting learning adversely – there is no need to rate every descriptor	Please tick*			Frequency rating			Comments
		B	E	A	High	Medium	Low	
1	Keeping things in mind							
2	Remembering processes/sequences							
3	Remembering images and symbols							
4	Plan and do (completing written tasks)							
5	Processing sounds							
6	Remembering sounds							
7	Matching phoneme to grapheme							
8	Slow pace							

#	Category				
9	Reading – speed/fluency/comprehension				
10	Spelling				
9	Laterality (right from left)				
10	Core stability				
11	Fine and gross motor skills				
12	Proprioception (awareness of body in space)				
13	Co-ordination				
14	Balance				
15	Concepts of number				
16	Algebra				
17	Complex calculations				
18	Proximity				
19	Relating to peers				

(Continued)

Table 3.1 (Continued)

	Current attainment in your subject	Please tick*			Comments
	Rate behaviours affecting learning adversely – there is no need to rate every descriptor	B	E	A	
		Frequency rating			
		High	Medium	Low	
20	Playing				
21	Conversations				
22	Appropriate responses				
23	Awareness of social cues				
24	Range of interests				
25	Eye contact				
26	Social understanding and interaction				
27	Non-verbal and verbal communication				

28	Imagination and flexible thinking				
29	Blurting				
30	Turn taking				
31	Lack of participation				
32	Fidgety				
33	Day dreaming				
34	Focus				
35	Reluctance to switch activities				
36	Difficulty sitting				
37	Constant fidgeting				
38	Out of seat				
39	Taps and drums				

(Continued)

Table 3.1 (Continued)

	Rate behaviours affecting learning adversely – there is no need to rate every descriptor	Current attainment in your subject	Please tick*			Frequency rating			Comments
			B	E	A	High	Medium	Low	
40	Dislikes getting dirty hands								
41	Throws very hard								
42	Breaks pencil when writing								
43	Verbal comprehension								
44	Expressive language								
45	Pragmatics								
46	Semantics								
47	Articulation								

Table 3.2 Needs Matrix Action Plan

Number	Difficulty	Strategy (DR GOPTA)	Cross curricular goal

Chapter 4: What are core deficits?

Table 4.1 Core deficit – Specialist Report Digest

Specialist Report Digest		
Pupil Name	**Date of Report**	
Notes about baselines		
Subject specific concerns		
Cognitive strengths		
Are there suggestions about the use of specific materials, books or technology?		
Has this added to your understanding of the pupil and their family?		

Table 4.2 Core deficit – class overview

Name	EP	SaLT	OT	Other	Working memory	Slow procesing	Phonological Processing	Fine motor

Chapter 5: What is multi-sensory teaching?

Table 5.1 Sensory audit of the classroom/teaching space

Environment	Does this vary depending on the activity?	How often does it vary?	Can this be improved?	Action
Lights: source and level				
Temperature				
Seating				
Space between furniture				
Height and angle of tables				
Use of headphones				
Orientation of room				
Air circulation				
Time spent in one attitude				
Seating plan				
View of the boards				
Access to basic materials				

Table 5.2 Sensory audit of the classroom routines

Routine	Issue	Adaption for All
Lesson changes/bells		
Greeting		
Seating		
Lining up for breaks		
Dressing for PE		
Packing kit		
Homework bag		
Assembly		
Eating lunch		
Clearing up		

Chapter 6: Who are DR GOPTA and MR CHUFFI?

Table 6.1 Classroom Talk Audit

	I use ... Often = O; Sometimes = S; Never = N	O/S/N Rating
Introduce, repeat and re-enforce important spoken vocabulary	Be selective and explicit when introducing new words.	
	Break down words into syllables verbal and visual (presentation).	
	Explain where the word comes from.	
	Explore and explain how it is linked to this and other subjects.	
	Can it be visually represented – pictogram?	
	Is prefix and suffix helpful to note?	
	Use word often and consistently – both say and show.	
	Offer all of the above more than once using same language to avoid confusion.	
	Reward correct use of word rather than correct spelling out of context.	

Encourage active listening	Show attention		
	Show empathy		
	Manage non-verbal communication		
	Paraphrase		
	Summarise		
	Play barrier games		
	Play word or phrase bingo		
Questioning	Show attention		
	Show empathy and acceptance		
	Manage non-verbal communication		
	Paraphrase		
	Summarise		
	Play barrier games		
	Reward active listening		
Encourage Speaking	Provide opportunities for pupils to talk, comment, reflect and question.		
	Don't allow seating plan and classroom geography to create random constraints.		
	Use 'mantle of the expert'.		

(Continued)

Table 6.1 (Continued)

	I use . . .	Often = O; Sometimes = S; Never = N	A/S/N	Rating
Vary listening focus/voice	Pupil voice			
	TA			
	Books on tape			
	Radio and podcasts			
	Community voices			
Address grammar in speech by offering	Corrections			
	Explanations			
	Rewards			
Vary volume, tone and register	Model appropriate tone and register			
	Manage volume			
	Identify inside outside, individual and group voices			

Table 6.2 Vocabulary planning

Opportunities	Behaviour	Opportunity
Vocabulary	Be selective and explicit when introducing new words.	
	Break down words into syllables verbal and visual presentation.	
	Explain where the word comes from.	
	Explore and explain how it is linked to this and other subjects.	
	Can it be visually represented – pictogram?	
	Are common prefixes and suffixes helpful to explore?	
	Use the word often and consistently – both say and show.	
	Offer all of the above repeatedly – come back to new words.	
	Reward pupil's use of the word in correct context.	

Table 6.3 Active listening

Opportunities	Behaviour	Opportunity
Encourage active listening	Show attention	
	Show empathy and acceptance	
	Manage non-verbal communication	
	Paraphrase	
	Summarise	
	Play barrier games	
	Reward active listening	

Table 6.4 Asking questions

Opportunities	Behaviour	Opportunity
Questions	Explain open and closed questions.	
	Use mixture of open and closed questions.	
	Vary thinking time for verbal responses (slow burners).	
	Reward useful pupil questions.	
	Provide visual cues for high-frequency questions.	

Table 6.5 Encouraging speaking

Opportunities	Behaviour	Opportunity
Encourage speaking	Provide opportunities for pupils to talk, comment, reflect and question.	
	Don't allow seating plan and classroom geography to create random constraints.	
	Use 'mantle of the expert'.	

Table 6.6 Varying listening

Opportunities	Behaviour	Opportunity
Vary listening focus/voice	Pupil voice	
	TA	
	Books on tape	
	Radio and podcasts	
	Community voices	

Table 6.7 Addressing grammar

Opportunities	Behaviour	Opportunity
Address grammar in speech by offering	Corrections	
	Explanations	
	Rewards	

Table 6.8 Varying volume

Opportunities	Behaviour	Opportunity		
Vary volume, tone and register	Model appropriate tone and register.			
	Manage volume			
	Identify inside, outside, individual and group voices.			

Table 6.9 Using resources

	Resources			
	Human	Material	Technological	Therapeutic
Standard				
Additional				

Table 6.10 Visual cues audit

Effective teaching	MR CHUFFI	Visual Cue
Making Links		
Risk Taking		
Cognitive Engagement		
Higher Level Thinking		
Checking Understanding		
Frequent Feedback		
Fostering Independence		

Table 6.11 Grouping

	Method of selection	Frequency		Rationale/impact
Random groups			M	
			R	
			C	
			H	
			U	
			FF	
			I	
Student selected			M	
			R	
			C	

T			
U			
FF			
I			
M			
R			
C			
T			
U			
FF			
I			

Teacher selected

Chapter 7: How can I work most effectively with Teaching Assistants?

Table 7.1 Teacher talk tally

Number of open questions	
Number of closed questions	
Number of instructions	
Phrases for praise	
Number of students praised	
Phrases for sanction	
Number of students sanctioned	
Phrases for checking understanding	
Phrases for dealing with the unexpected	

Minutes of silence	
Minutes of pupil talk/voice	
To what extent is my speech grammatically correct?	
Where do I speak from?	
Number of deliberate repetitions	
Number of requested repetitions	
Number of times I raise voice for attention	
Variation of tone and register	
Clarity of speech	
Pace of speech	

Table 7.2 Visual Cues Audit

MR CHUFFI		
Effective teaching		Visual cue
Making Links		
Risk Taking		
Cognitive Engagement		
Higher Level Thinking		
Checking Understanding		
Frequent Feedback		
Fostering Independence		

Table 7.3 In-class support practices

	In-class support practices	Never	Sometimes	Mostly	Always
1	I circulate in class rather than sit with identified pupils.				
2	Pupils know how to get my attention.				
3	I create visual aids/reminders in advance.				
4	I create visual aids and reminders in the classroom as required.				
5	I have a consistent support strategy which removes or reduces barriers to learning.				
6	I highlight and emphasise key points.				
7	I check before I chastise.				
8	I encourage risk-taking in learning.				
9	I enable teacher engagement/involvement with my target pupils.				
10	I record and share information about learning.				

(Continued)

Table 7.3 (Continued)

	In-class support practices	Never	Sometimes	Mostly	Always
11	I chunk tasks.				
12	I read for pupils.				
13	I scribe for pupils.				
14	I rephrase and re-explain tasks to pupils.				
15	I assist with behaviour management for all pupils.				
16	I use agreed strategies to manage the behaviour of target pupils.				
17	I have a toolkit for supporting memory.				
18	I have a sensory toolkit for supporting pupils with DCD and SID.				

Chapter 8: How do I share good practice?

Table 8.1 Compare SEND and non-SEND pupils

MR CHUFFI agenda	SEND pupils	Non-SEND pupils	Comment or support DR GOPTA
Making Links			
Risk Taking			
Cognitive Engagement			
Checking Understanding			
Higher Level thinking			
Frequent Feedback			
Fostering Independence			

Chapter 9: How do I implement change?

Table 9.1 Implementing change

What do I want?		
What am I doing?		
How does it feel?		
What went wrong?		
What feedback is there?		
What am I doing to support myself?		

Index

Note: Page numbers in italics indicate figures and in bold indicate tables on the corresponding pages.

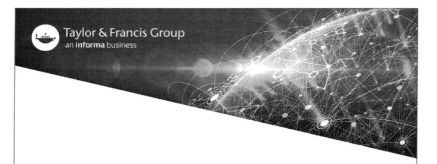

Printed in Great Britain
by Amazon

49114493R00108